FLAVOURS OF
LANCASHIRE

THE FOOD AND FOLK OF THE OLD COUNTY

H.J. GRUNDY
FRESH
MUSSELS
£ 2.50
TWO KILO
SACK
1/2 SACK £ 1.50
FRESH
CREVETTES
£ 2.50
100 GRAMS

FLAVOURS OF LANCASHIRE
THE FOOD AND FOLK OF THE OLD COUNTY

MALCOLM GREENHALGH

First published in 2006
by Palatine Books,
Carnegie House,
Chatsworth Road
Lancaster LA1 4SL
www.palatinebooks.com

British Library Cataloguing-in-Publication data
A catalogue record for this book is available from the British Library

ISBN 10: 1-874181-39-X
ISBN 13: 978-1-874181-39-2

Designed and typeset by Carnegie Book Production
www.carnegiebookproduction.com
Printed and bound in the UK by Alden Press

CONTENTS

Malcolm Greenhalgh was born in Bolton, raised at Kirkham and Preston, studied biology at Lancaster University, did research on the Ribble estuary for his PhD and lectured up to his fortieth birthday. In the last twenty years he has been a freelance writer specialising on wildlife. He has published about fifteen books, the last of which, *The Wild Salmon* (Merlin Unwin Books), describes the natural history of this fascinating fish. March 2007 sees the publication of a magnum opus, *A Guide to the Freshwater Life of Britain and Northern Europe* (HarperCollins). Despite his wanderings to foreign coasts, lakes and rivers, Malcolm remains first and foremost a Lancastrian and he is now working on books describing the history and natural history of his home region. A new book, *The Ribble: A Natural and Local History*, will be published by Carnegie Publishing in 2007.

IMPORTANT NOTE

Please note that this is not primarily a recipe book. The book is about food and people, and where there are recipes they are Lancastrian recipes. So please do not expect to be told how to make pastry or roast a leg of lamb or boil carrots. These are in every cookery book and are not repeated here. Do not feel that, when a recipe is given, it is writ in letters of stone. Too many people treat recipes rather like experiments in school chemistry, so that when it says 'half a teaspoon' or 'three quarters of a pound' they must be measured with great precision. Recipes are simply guides which you may modify as you will.

Of course only a fool wanders far from basic recipes.

About twenty years ago, on a bleak, wet Lancashire winter's day, I decided to make that wonderfully comforting dish, steak and kidney pudding. 'Remind me,' I said as the wife headed off to work, 'suet pastry. Two to one, isn't it?' 'Yes,' she said.

I began to mix one part flour to two parts suet but it felt all wrong. So I phoned the wife at work. 'Two flour to one suet, you idiot!' she said.

So I added extra flour to make the proportions correct and found that now I had enough suet pastry to make four steak and kidney puddings. So I went down to the butchers, bought another three pounds of steak and kidney. I went to the fishmongers and bought another dozen oysters. And when the wife returned from her labours, she found four steak and kidney puddings steaming away on top of the cooker.

It was no problem. We ate one that night and when they were cold I froze the others. And on three other bleak, wet Lancashire days I took one from the freezer and just boiled it. Now that's what I call proper convenience food!

TEMPERATURES, VOLUMES, WEIGHTS AND COOKING

ALTHOUGH THIS BOOK IS MAINLY ABOUT Lancastrian food and the people who used to – and still do – eat and produce it, and not simply a list of recipes, having some recipes or ways of cooking the food is unavoidable. Indeed, some readers might like to try cooking some of the 'flavours of Lancashire' that they have never cooked before. However I do not want the book to be cluttered up with oven temperatures in different scales and measures in various weights and volumes. Instead the various measures are listed below and may be referred to when necessary.

Temperature

	Gas	° F	° C
Water freezes at		32	0
Water simmers at		185–205	85–95
Water boils at		212	100
Very slow oven	½–1	250–300	120–150
Slow oven	2–3	300–350	150–175
Moderate oven	4	350–375	175–190
Moderately hot oven	5–6	375–400	190–205
Hot oven	7	400–425	205–220
Very hot oven *	8	over 425	over 220

* Rarely used; most domestic ovens do not go above 450F, 245C.

Note that, although some recipe books give quite precise temperatures (and cooking times), ovens do vary; some are 'faster' ovens than others. Temperatures and cooking times should therefore be used as a guide, not as a decree set in concrete.

Volume

1 litre = 1 ¾ pints
1 pint = 20 fluid ounces = 570 cc
1 teaspoon = 5cc (cc is the same as ml)

Weight

1 kg = 2.2 lbs
1 lb = 454 g (often rounded down to 450 g)
1 oz = 28 g (often rounded down to 25 g)

INTRODUCTION

U P TO LATE IN THE TWENTIETH CENTURY, most of the history that we might have read in books and magazines, or listened to on radio, or watched on television, was about kings and queens, of battles and wars between people who disagreed with each other, and of captains who controlled and directed industry. Only relatively rarely did history concern itself with ordinary people, and then it usually treated them as canon-fodder, serfs and slaves, or as a mass nuisance that got in the way of government instead of following their 'rightful' role as acquiescent provider of labour. In recent years, however, there has been a boom in researching family history and in local historians investigating their communities. This book a contribution to this new sort of history, for it is about Lancashire food, its history and its unique recipes. It is about the food that would have been eaten by the forebears of all of us lucky enough to be born into ordinary Lancashire families. It includes traditional food that some of us still enjoy today, as well as some of the newer 'flavours of Lancashire'.

Most history books highlight the foods devoured by those in authority or of great wealth, for what they ate, especially at grand dinners, were recorded in detail with pen and paper. No one was interested enough to record it officially for posterity, so it is largely through stories and recipes passed from generation to generation that we know about the food placed on humbler tables.

1

Food fit for a King

Whalley Abbey was built by the River Calder, close to its confluence with the Ribble, its foundation stone being set in place on 12 June 1296 by Henry de Lacy. Though consecrated ten years later in 1306, the entire magnificence of the abbey complex took 142 years to complete. The abbot led a brotherhood of up to thirty monks as well as a number of resident servants. Important people who were travelling through the Ribble valley would have stayed there for at least one night, for suitable accommodation was then rare and being out at night dangerous. Henry VIII dissolved the abbey in 1537 and its last abbot, John Parslew, was hanged just outside Whalley village.

The detailed accounts of the abbey reveal that the relatively small Abbey community devoured about 130 cows, 60 calves, 120 sheep and 30 lambs every year. It is important to remember that this amount of red meat was not eaten over 365 days, but on only 235 days, for 130 days were Days of Obligation, when eating red meat was not permitted. On those days, however, the community was permitted to eat fish and, sometimes, poultry. Fish was readily available, for the abbey had fishing rights to harvest the large numbers of salmon and sea trout that swam in the Ribble, and they built a fish-farm on the flood plain of the Calder to provide other species of edible fish such as carp, bream and pike. These foods, together with vegetables and cereals, were produced locally. The abbey also imported from afar huge quantities of wine, dried fruits such as raisins, dates and figs, a wide range of spices, and sugar, then a most expensive commodity. At least sixty per cent of the very large income of the abbey was spent on food and drink.

The ruins of the gateway at Whalley Abbey.

It seems that Salley (Sawley) Abbey, a few miles up the Ribble valley from Whalley, was equally extravagant. In 1381 each of its thirty monks and novices drank 300 gallons of ale and, despite a large income from rents throughout the region, that year the abbey was able to provide only five shillings and eight pence (31p) for charity.

We can but guess at what the poor peasants living in the Ribble valley had to eat in the fourteenth, fifteenth and sixteenth centuries.

In August 1617 King James I and his retinue spent three days as guests of the de Hoghton family at Hoghton Tower between Preston and Blackburn. Every day Chefs Morris and Miller and their twelve assistants prepared a dinner that could only be described as gargantuan! Among those sitting down to dinner on Sunday the 17th of August was Nicholas Assheton of Downham in the Ribble Valley. Assheton kept a detailed diary of his life as a hunter and glutton (gourmet would be too kind a term!) and his published *Journal* lists the dishes on offer:

First Course

Pullets	Goose roasted
Boiled Capon	Rabbits cold
Mutton boiled	Jiggits* of Mutton boiled
Boiled Chickens	Snipe pye
Shoulder of Mutton roast	Breast of Veal boiled
Ducks boiled	Capons roast
Loin of Veal roast	Pullet
Pullets	Beef roast †
Haunch of Venison roast	Tongue pye cold
Burred Capon	Sprod boiled ‡
Pasty of Venison hot	Herons roast cold
Roast Turkey	Curlew pye cold
Veal burred §	Mince pye hot
Swan roast, one, and one for to-morrow	Custards
Chicken pye hot	Pig roast

Second Course

Hot Pheasant, one and one for the King.	Hot Herons roast, three of a dish
Quails, six for the King	Lamb roast
Partridge	Gammon of Bacon
Poults	Pigeons roast
Artichoke pye	Made dish #
Chickens	Chicken burred
Curlews roast	Pear tart
Peas buttered	Pullets and grease **
Rabbits	Dried tongues
Duck	Turkey pye
Plovers	Pheasant pye
Red Deer pye	Pheasant tart
Pig burred	Hog's cheek dried
	Turkey chicks cold.

* A jiggit was a haunch, usually of mutton or venison, spit-roasted in front of the fire.

† It was here that James I is said to have knighted a loin of beef and exclaimed, 'Rise! Sir Loin!'

‡ 'Sprod' is an old Lancashire name for sea trout. This delicious fish runs the rivers in summer from the sea in order to spawn in late autumn.

§ 'Burred' meant that the animal has been split open and could be laid out flat for cooking, rather like a spatchcocked chichen.

A 'made dish' was one contained several ingredients. Veal and ham pie, with boiled eggs through the middle, is one form of made dish, as would be chicken and mushroom pie.

** Pulets and grease were young chickens cooked in butter.

Later that evening a similar meal was put in front of the King and his lords and this included some dishes not devoured at dinner (then eaten at midday): 'Umble pye', 'Cold Neat's tongue pye', 'Neat's tongue roast', and 'Wild Boar pye'. Umble (or humble or hummel) is a red deer stag that fails to grow antlers, whilst 'neat' is an old name for an ox.

The magnificent drive to Hoghton Tower, along which King James I rode to dinner.

Ordinary people were not invited to the party, so we have no written record of what they had to eat. Who cared anyway? Few ordinary folk were literate, and in any case they had no time to write down their menu.

Parson James Woodforde was not a Lancastrian, but his diaries from 1758 to 1802 described a meal that was probably very similar to the sort of meal laid before most Lancashire parsons and major land-owners at the time. Woodforde described a small dinner that his wife organised for a few friends one day in 1794.

For the first course the table was laid with dishes of stewed tench, mutton stew and mutton pie, a couple of roast chickens, a ham, some boiled beef, mashed potatoes, unspecified root vegetables, some custard puddings and a bowl of veal soup. When that lot had been consumed a second course was laid on the table, which included a fricassee of rabbit, two roast ducks, a trifle and a blancmange, cheesecakes, a bowl of macaroni and a plate of raspberry tarts. When the servants had cleared the remains of all that away the parson and his guests ended their simple repast with fresh peaches, nectarines and plums.

'AN OLD MARSHSIDE (SOUTHPORT) SAYING: A FAMILY WITH A PIG, TWO SACKS OF POTATOES AND A BAG OF SALT NEED NOT FEAR THE WINTER'

No similar eighteenth-century menu is available from a simple Lancashire family, though Nicholas Blundell, who lived at Crosby, gives us a list of the expenses incurred for his father's funeral on 6

August 1702 in his diaries. On spices he spent 6 shillings 11½ pence (almost 35p), on four dozen bottle of wine £4, and on a barrel-and-a-half of beer £2 8s (£2.40). The list of meat consumed by family and friends included poultry (13s 4d; 66p), two pigs (7s; 35p), mutton (£1 1s; £1.05), hams (3s; 15p), 'Flesh Pies, Tarts, Custards, Etc.' (£1 5s; £1.25), and bread and butter. His expenses include a separate item costing two pounds: 'Bread given to the Tenants & Neighbours but not to the Beggars'. Marie Antoinette at least let them eat cake!

Three years after Parson Woodforde's dinner party a slim volume called *The State of the Poor* was published (in 1797). It describes the finances of a typical farm labourer who earned between three and four shilling (15–20p) per week. Then a loaf of bread cost a halfpenny, a pound of butter nine pence, and the wages were spent – as far as food is concerned – on tea, sugar, bread and potatoes. The potato was then a 'standing dish', in other words an important staple, in northern England. There is no mention of meat, nor fruit. That does not mean to say that the eighteenth-century farm labourer and his family did not eat meat or fruit. It is simply that little, if any, was purchased. Most ordinary folk in Lancashire then lived in the country (see page 8) and would have had a vegetable plot where they were able to grow onions, garlic (that we erroneously consider to have come to us recently from the Mediterranean), leeks, peas and beans, cabbages, carrots and turnips. They may have had an apple tree and perhaps a couple of blackcurrant bushes. They would have had a few hens scratching a living outside the back door. Many ordinary cottagers kept a pig, which was fattened up to be slaughtered in autumn (see page 68). Those living on the coast may also have been able to add fish and shellfish to their diets, and those living near to rivers or lakes freshwater fish, though all fisheries including the shore were then privately owned and rigorously preserved (page 108). Most other wildlife, including rabbits, game and wildfowl, was also protected by landowners, though occasionally a rabbit or mallard might ends its days in a cottager's pot.

The country dweller also obtained animal protein from sources that the twenty-second-century Lancastrian would never contemplate.

In winter, when the hens were not laying eggs and the store of salted pork was dwindling, small birds were sought, especially on the flat, wet, peaty farmland and grassy saltmarshes around the Ribble estuary, with snares locally called 'pantles'. Pantles were made of twisted horse-hair, the main line or 'rudge' being twelve yards in length and twenty hairs in thickness, and into this, the nooses, of one or two hairs, and known as 'guilders' were woven in pairs, about three inches apart. The 'rudge' was stretched three inches from the

'BREAD GIVEN TO TENANTS AND NEIGHBOURS, BUT NOT TO THE BEGGARS'

ground, and fastened to four pegs called 'nebs', fourteen inches long, one at each end, and the other two dividing it into three equal lengths or 'bows'. Putting guelders for the first time was called 'eyeing', and setting them after they have been used was 'tilling'. Before setting a pantle the ground had to be prepared by the fowlers shuffling along sideways, with the feet close together, so that they trampled a strip of grass about a foot in width, that in the darkness would have some resemblance to a narrow channel of water.

How many inhabitants of Hesketh Bank, Banks, Freckleton or Lytham today would know what a pantle, rudge, guilder and neb was used for?

Skylarks were taken in large numbers, together with snipe, meadow pipits and the occasional larger species such as teal. In 1972 I spoke to an old man who lived near Tarleton. He recalled that, before the First World War, he and his father set many pantles in the wet meadows of Martin Mere. 'Most of our catch was skylarks, with a few snipe. All the catch went to market in Preston on Saturday with the vegetables from our market garden,' he told me. More recently, shrimper Peter Rimmer from Marshside described how, when food was getting scarce in winter, people would go out onto the Ribble saltmarshes to catch starlings for the pot. 'But don't starlings taste bitter?' I asked. 'It was protein. They had to eat them or go without,' was his reply.

It is important to remember, when looking at traditional Lancashire fare, that ours was a very poor county until the coming of the Industrial Revolution. Wealthy religious foundations, land-owners and the like were rare. The majority of Lancastrians had virtually nothing. For instance, in 1515 the wealthiest county in England was Essex and it was worth £102 per 1000 acres. The average English county was worth £66 per 1000 acres, the West Riding of Yorkshire £11.30, and poor Lancashire ... only £3.80. It was then the poorest of the 38 counties. By 1693 things were little better, for then Lancashire came 35 out of 38 in the league table. Then most of the towns we see today were mere villages and people lived on the land.

'THE MAJORITY OF LANCASTRIANS HAD VIRTUALLY NOTHING'

Much of the countryside that makes up Lancashire and from which most of the population had to eke out a living was agriculturally unproductive. About 60,000 acres was mossland: a mosaic of peaty fenland, bog, heather moor and scrub. Today almost every acre of that mossland has been drained and turned into rich arable farmland. To the east the county is dominated by steep-sided moorland slopes with a summit plateau often covered by peaty, inhospitable blanket bog. On some of the moors we can still see the remains of stone hovels from which people tried to make a living. Should the staples of

oats or potatoes fail, a family living in remote corners of the county would face starvation; a village thus afflicted would face famine. The county itself produced little surplus to feed failures, there was no spare money to buy food in from wealthy counties such as Essex, and transport in the country was fairly primitive.

The wet summer of 1799 resulted in the cereal crop failing across the western Fylde (as, incidentally, happened in 2004 throughout much of Lancashire, though few people will have noticed). Then the potato crop succumbed to blight. The desperate shortage of food in the 1799–80 winter was relieved by providence wrecking a ship laden with dried peas on the beach of Blackpool, then only a few cottages (its population two years later in 1801 was only 473). Shipwrecked peas were the staple that winter. One old fisherman was reported to have said that, 'we couldn't stomach 'em for years after … Still th'peas were a blessing. We should ha' clemmed, but for that wreck …'

Rural Lancastrians had their staples like oats and potatoes that dominated their diet, but they were capable of improvisation. If something could be cooked, they cooked and ate it. In spring, when fresh food was getting scarce, the leaves of wild plants such as nettles, dandelions and Good King Henry would go into the pot. A dead rabbit or pigeon might be brought in by the back door and turned into a nourishing, tasty dish. One of my grandmothers, Ada Greenhalgh,

was particularly innovative in the kitchen. When I was nine years old I shot a moorhen with my catapult in a pond close to Kirkham. She took my prize and, with some pearl barley, carrot, turnip and a small onion, turned it into a delicious dish that triggered my interest in food and cookery. But what she did in 1955 was nothing special: most women in rural eighteenth-century Lancashire would have improvised with little, unexpected extras that turned up from time to time.

But then, from the middle of the eighteenth century, a series of Enclosure Acts drove thousands of cottagers from their land. At the same time the towns of south and east Lancashire began to be the centres of industry. Work became concentrated in factories. Factories needed lots of coal to produce the steam that drove the machinery, so the towns close to the Lancashire coalfields grew rapidly, dragging thousands of people in from the countryside.

In 1701 Bolton had a population of less than a thousand; by 1801 it had grown to 19,500, by 1901 to 168,215, and by 1911 to 180,815. In 1801 only about 15,000 people lived in Blackburn and Darwen; by 1901 there were 158,000. Burnley had a population of barely 2,000 in 1790, had grown to 5,200 by 1801 and peaked at 103,186 in 1921. The town of Preston, now a city and the administrative centre of Lancashire, had only about 6,000 inhabitants in 1770 and 12,000 in 1801; by 1881 the population had exploded to 104,012, and by 1911 to 133,052. In 1819 there were 344 cotton mills in south Lancashire; by 1839 there were 1,815 mills and people had quit the countryside to work in the towns. In 1801, 74% of Lancastrians still lived and worked in the countryside; by 1891, 94% of Lancastrians were town-dwellers.

The slum dwellings and the Coronation Street two-up-and-two-down terraced house had no vegetable plot for growing a few vegetables. There was no room to keep a pig or a few chickens that might scratch a living from around the back door, for beyond the terraced house were more identical terraced houses set out in long rows, with cobbled streets between them and brooding over all the shadow of the mill. No longer was it possible to nip outside in spring

Those who were born in country cottages just before the Local Enclosure Act might have spent the rest of their lives in back-to-back terraces like these, on Plank Lane, Leigh.

to gather young nettle leaves or in autumn to pick some blackberries. The man of the house could no longer pop out at dusk to snare a rabbit, for there were no rabbits in the middle of 'urbia'. Even the fuel needed for heating and cooking changed when families moved from countryside to town. The country dweller might gather wood or cut peat for nothing or for a small charge. The town dweller could not and fuel, in the form of coal, had to be bought.

Wages in the mills and factories were low. So buying the staple foods, wheat flour or oatmeal and potatoes, took up most of the disposable income after fuel and accommodation had been paid for, just as had been the situation among the rural poor. Bought meat was mostly either offal or salted pork or bacon. The water available for drinking through those decades during which the towns were growing rapidly was often loaded with bacteria that caused diseases such a cholera and dysentery. So tea made with boiling water or beer became the standard drinks (see page 24). An arduous lifestyle demanded lots of energy and imported refined, granulated cane sugar became increasingly important, either dissolved in tea or in cakes and puddings. This was urban Lancashire food, borne of a hard life style and low income. But there were not the extras provided by the open countryside that, with ingenuity, could be turned into a nourishing meal.

So, asked Colin Spencer in his book *A History of British Food*, 'What happened to our heritage of rural cooking? The cottagers and farm labourers who moved to the industrial towns had no means to buy food or even to cook it, so those habitual daily recipes which had been a central part of their life must have been lost within a few years. These people for the most part were illiterate, so the recipes that had once passed on from generation to generation now vanished. No other European country suffered this experience ...'

Spencer is exaggerating a little, for most Lancashire families could still afford the basics of potatoes, flour and bread, and most did have a fire on which they could put a kettle and cooking pot. And those still living in the country did continue to cook and produce the old Lancashire dishes. What did affect cooking in the urban population was the growth of pie shops, pea stalls, fish and chip shops and bakers' shops. Many families stopped cooking, especially on workdays, and bought the new convenience food. J. K. Walton highlighted this in his book *Lancashire: A Social History*: 'Women in Barrow [-in-Furness, that was part of Lancashire up to 1974] and Lancaster made their money go further by baking their own bread and cooking nourishing stews and vegetable dishes, whereas cotton-workers' families subsisted largely on shop bread, shop-made pies and cakes, fry-ups and fish and chips, more expensive and less nutritious.' Canned foods were convenient but also added to the cost of food. Though the canning of meat, fruit and vegetables began in the late 1800s, canned foods really became an important part of the urban worker's diet from the 1920s. Some families stopped eating freshly prepared vegetables and fruit, choosing canned garden or processed peas, baked beans, cling peaches and mandarin oranges instead. Such convenience cost more money and lost out on nutrients.

'THIS WAS URBAN LANCASHIRE FOOD, BORNE OF A HARD LIFE STYLE AND LOW INCOME'

Today the chippy, Indian and Chinese 'takeaway', and pie and cake and bread shop are still dominant features in the diet of many urban Lancastrians.

RATIONING

In January 1940 allowances for 'things that were on the ration' were: bacon 4 oz, sugar 12 oz, tea 2 oz, cooking fat (lard or dripping) 4 oz, margarine 2 oz and butter 2 oz per person per week. In May 1941 cheese was 'put on the ration' at 1 oz per person per week. Meat and eggs were also rationed, and many imported foods that we take for granted today, such as bananas and oranges, were not available at all. It has been said that during rationing, people were fitter than they are today!

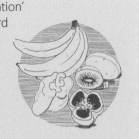

S. Mintz suggested in the book *Tasting Food, Tasting Freedom*, that 'War is probably the single most powerful instrument of dietary change in human experience.'

That is certainly true of the Second World War. The end of rationing in the early 1950s was quickly followed by the income of the Lancashire worker increasing in real terms so that families had a surplus that could be spent on food. Instead of the children getting the top of a boiled egg for Sunday breakfast and parents getting the rest, people could afford to have an egg – even two eggs – each. Then there appeared in shops and in the increasingly dominant supermarkets a range of foods that was undreamt of in the 1930s and 1940s. Frozen prawns and farmed salmon. Avocados, aubergines, globe artichokes and sweet peppers. Bananas, kiwi fruits, melons and mangoes. Poussin, guinea fowl and Gressingham duck. Pasta and Carmargue rice. Breakfast cereals in a bewildering range. Fruit juices, yoghurts and semi-skimmed milk. Semi-skimmed milk! That's milk with some of the energy (fat) taken out of it! Can you imagine a Lancashire mill worker or coal miner asking for semi-skimmed milk in the 1930s!

Developments in agriculture led to formerly expensive food becoming inexpensive in the second half of the twentieth century. In the 1930s chicken was a special treat for a special day; by 2000 it was cheap everyday food. A turkey is now not just for Christmas. The breeding of more productive strains and the use of pesticides and herbicides resulted in the staples of flour, bread and potatoes ceasing to make a major hole in the money a family has available for food. Today some families spend more on a bottle of wine from the supermarket than they do on a week's supply of bread and potatoes. Wine? The only wine that most Lancastrians drank in the 1930s was either tonic wine or communion wine!

Then came along TV chefs who demonstrated how viewers might prepare the dishes that they enjoyed at their local restaurant or on a recent holiday in Torremolinos. People no longer sought energy-rich foods (though the present consumption of chocolate bars might suggest otherwise). Nor did they want meals based on cheap cuts of meat, that take a long time to cook, or offal. Slowly real Lancashire food was replaced by a new, late-twentieth-century British diet that is itself now in decline.

SCHOOL DINNERS

Recently a well-known TV chef created a rumpus over the quality of meals served up to the nation's children at lunchtime. Greasy beef burgers, chips, chicken bits laced with E-numbers and other concoctions have been blamed, in part at least, on the obesity of so many children. The fact that the little dears are not allowed to walk to and from school or to burn up those calories by 'playing out' is to some extent overlooked. But what Jamie Oliver's campaign forgets is that we used to have balanced, healthy school dinners. The local authorities and schools stopped providing them.

Although we used to moan about them (moaning gave us a sense of togetherness) our school dinners in the late 1950s and early 1960s were excellent. The main course always had real meat: boiled beef, beef stew, cottage pie, lamb chops, real boiled ham, roast pork, liver (Ughh! But we ate it!), and, on Friday, cod or haddock baked, not fried. With that went boiled, mashed or roasted potatoes (never chips) and a freshly cooked vegetable. Puddings included jam roly-poly, Bakewell tart, treacle sponge and, best of all, cornflake tart. These were served with a liberal helping of good-old custard. One day every week there was a milk pudding: semolina, rice, tapioca ('frog spawn') served with jam.

Did we really dislike these well-cooked lunches? The proof is in the eating. Few boys would refuse a second helping and particularly hungry boys would find their way into the two sittings and thereby enjoy two lunches!

Today supermarkets are reducing shelf-space for fresh foods and cooking ingredients and putting chilled cabinets and deep freezers full of packets of ready-to-eat meals in their place. Yorkshire puddings, roast potatoes, meat with gravy, battered cod in parsley sauce, pancakes for Shrove Tuesday, Aunt Annie's authentic country crumble. Just remove the packing and plonk them in the microwave. And note the warning: 'Danger, after being heated this product is hot!' Some families do not go even that far. Cooking takes time and creates washing up. So more and more leave home in the early evening to enjoy the delights of pub-chains, Burger King, MacDonalds, KFC or Pizza Hut food.

A class of Nutrition and Cookery students in a college of further education in the heart of Lancashire was given a list of the ingredients they had to bring to the next practical class. They were going to make that old Lancashire favourite, a plate custard, with a pastry case containing the filling made from eggs, milk, sugar and vanilla extract (see page 140). One student turned up with a can of Bird's custard and a note from her mother. 'There's no point in making custard and I'm not wasting money on buying the ingredients. Tinned custard is just as good!'

'Danger, after being heated this product is hot!'

How sad it will be if the art of cooking is lost. And for those of us who are proud to be Lancastrian, how sad it will be if our food heritage disappears for ever.

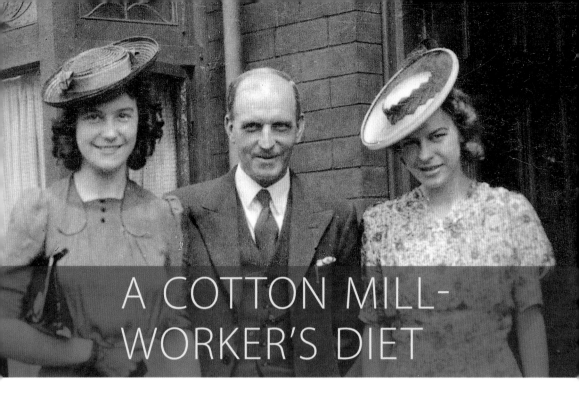

A COTTON MILL-
WORKER'S DIET

Bert Haslam with his daughters Doris (my mother) and Irene. Five and a half days were spent in the cotton mill; Saturday afternoon was for the garden; and Sunday was given over to church, for Bert was Vicar's Warden at St George the Martyr's church in Bolton.

MY GRANDFATHER ON MY MOTHER'S SIDE of the family was Herbert (Bert) Haslam. Born in 1890, he went into the cotton mill as soon as he could leave school, served in the later stages of the First World War (when he was awarded the Military Medal for bravery, rescuing injured comrades whilst under fire), and returned to work in the mill until his retirement at the age of 67. His life was a busy one, for he was a keen gardener and also churchwarden of St George-the-Martyr's church at Daubhill (pronounced 'Dobble') on the south side of Bolton. His church duties took up all Sunday; the mill took up five-and-a-half of the other six days.

Before he went to bed, my mother told me (on 6 April 2006) as she recalled the late 1920s and 1930s, he put a heavy pan containing coarse oatmeal, water and lots of salt onto the dying coal fire, and at five o'clock on the six mornings that he went to work he warmed up and then ate this oat gruel. The mill he worked in, Winder and McLean's at Great Lever, was three miles away from home and he made that journey on foot, no matter what the weather. Then, having arrived at work, he ate a couple of slices of bread and jam that had also been prepared the previous evening.

Work commenced at seven-thirty and continued to noon with only a short break for tea. The mill provided the hot water; the workers brought their own tea. He had a small metal box that was divided down the middle. One half of this box held dry tea-leaves, the other side contained white sugar. So at morning and afternoon break times and with his lunch, Bert drank a pint pot of sweet, black, milkless tea.

Lunch, or dinner as it was and still is often called in Lancashire, was the same for each of the five days, Monday to Friday. It consisted of a home-made potato pie, sometimes with a little meat, that Bert carried to the mill in a large white-spotted red cloth. There were no facilities for warming up food in the mill, so this pie was eaten cold. Those workers who lived close to the mill were often more fortunate. They too often ate a potato and meat pie for lunch, but that might be hot and carried round to the mill by one of their children who had gone home for their lunch from school.

Work ended ten hours after it began, at five-thirty. Bert then walked the three-miles home, getting there around six-thirty. The evening meal (or 'tea') was dominated by carbohydrates: bread, potatoes, sweet cakes and sugared tea with a tiny amount of meat or cheese. Bert probably used around 6,000 calories in his long day and his diet reflected this.

A century earlier, in 1832, John Burnett described the daily routine of a Manchester mill worker who lived just round the corner from the mill.

He awoke at five o'clock on six mornings every week. He had a drink of sugared tea and then set off for the mill. Work commenced at six o'clock but stopped at eight. Then the mill worker returned home for a breakfast of tea and bread before heading back to work. At noon he went home for his dinner of boiled potatoes with melted lard poured over them. Sometimes there might also be a scrap of fatty bacon. By one o'clock he was back at work. At six o'clock he returned home to eat a final meal of bread, washed down with sweet tea.

'WHY IS MY DINNER NO DINNER?'

That was the cry of Henry Hobson, manufacturer and purveyor of fine boots to the people of Salford, when his daughter put boiled tongue in front of him instead of roast pork, in the book and film, *Hobson's Choice*. For the middle class businessmen or tradesmen of Lancashire in the first half of the twentieth century, dinner (what we now often call lunch) was the main meal of the day and eaten at around one o'clock.

The dinner was usually of two courses. Meat or fish, with 'potatoes and two veg.' was the first course, and this would be followed by a substantial pudding. The diner would have been ready for his dinner. Unlike Henry Hobson, who spent the morning in bed recovering from the excesses of the previous evening in the Moonraker's Inn, most would have been in the office, factory or business since seven or eight in the morning, and after lunch they would be back working until five, six or seven o'clock in the evening.

One mill owner from Rochdale in the 1930s and 1940s used to have his secretary send a post card home at nine o'clock, to arrive by the eleven o'clock post, telling his wife precisely what time he would be back so that his dinner would be waiting for him.

A MINER'S
DAILY ROUTINE

The pit-head in Bickershaw colliery, Leigh, in about 1910. The canal in the foreground is the Leigh branch linking the Bridgwater and the Leeds & Liverpool canals. The horse and trap probably belonged to the mill owner.

BENJAMIN SMALL WAS BORN IN 1896 into a mining family in Glebe Street, Leigh. His father, James, was recorded on his birth certificate as a 'coal hewer' and he married the daughter of a 'coal hewer'. During the First World War he served with the 11th Manchester Regiment and was wounded twice.

Benjamin started working in the mine when he was thirteen years old and, other than during the war, he worked there until he retired at the age of 65. He usually worked night shifts cutting coal at the coalface. The shift commenced at 10.30pm and ended at 6am. However, his shift did not allow time for travel down the shaft in the cage or from the bottom of the shaft to the coalface. That he had to do in his own time and, because the coalface could be far from the bottom of the shaft along a maze of dark passages, he had to set out in plenty of time. So he would get the cage to the bottom of the pit shaft at about 10pm and get back to the surface at between 6.30 and 7am.

In *The Road to Wigan Pier*, George Orwell wrote of the Lancashire miners: 'the food they take with them is only a snack, usually bread-and-dripping and cold tea. They carry it in a flat tin called a snap-tin which they strap to their belts.' And that is what Benjamin did, though he ate jam butties more than bread-and-dripping.

When he got home Benjamin washed his sweat-and-coal dust encrusted body. It was not easy ridding the body of the all-pervading black dust. For two or three hours the nostrils would run with blackened mucus, and even after washing, until he had rubbed away the dust from his eyes, he looked as though he was wearing mascara. Then he drank a pint of tea before, in spring and summer, spending an hour tending his garden that supplied his family with fresh vegetables.

Orwell criticised Wigan miners who had garden plots for not bothering to grow vegetables, but he seems to have sought out the few. For the miners whom I got to know well before the Wigan–Leigh coalfield was closed down were not like Orwell described. If they lacked a garden then many had a local authority allotment (some had two allotments) where they kept a few hens and produced a wide range of vegetables. Some coursed rabbits and hares for the pot, with whippets or greyhounds. Others spent their free time fishing. Others playing and later in life watching rugby league. Life down t'pit may have been hard, dangerous and, in later life, debilitating. Yet away from work the life of a Lancashire miner was a rich and varied one.

'THE COAL MINER TOOK HIS FOOD DOWN THE PIT IN A SNAP-TIN. OTHER LANCASHIRE NAMES FOR LUNCH-TINS INCLUDE *BAIT-TIN*, *BUDGY*, *TOMMY-TIN* AND, AMONG LIVERPOOL DOCKERS, A *GROWLER*'

Benjamin Small on his vegetable plot.

SALT

'... if the salt have lost his savour, wherewith shall it be salted?.'
St Matthew 5:13.

WHILE NOT A FOOD ITSELF, salt has long been important in the taste of food, which is why the manufacturers of savoury snack and convenience foods have tended to load their products with high levels of salt. Salt was part of the Roman soldiers' wage, and we get the words 'salary' and 'saline' from the Latin for salt, *sal*. That corner of Lytham close to the Ribble estuary, Saltcotes, is so called because salt was once made there. The ancient track that crosses the Bowland fells between Hodder and Lune valleys is called Salter Fell Road. Heavily laden packhorses used this track as they carried salt from Cheshire to Penrith, Carlisle and other northern outposts. There were four bothies on this track where the packman and his load could shelter if foul weather suddenly struck: Higher, High, Mid and Lower Saltergs. Saltergs were 'salt shelters' and pronounced 'salter'.

But not all salt came from Cheshire. In the thirteenth century monks from Sawley (Salley) Abbey had the right to produce salt from seawater at North Meols (now called Churchtown, at the northern end of Southport). There they had grazing and they protected their land and salt works with an embankment to keep out the tides. Today that part of Meols is almost two miles from the highest tides.

By the sixteenth century salt-production was taking place at several sites on the Ribble and Wyre estuaries and the coast between Knott End and Lancaster. On neap tides (those that leave a large expanse of sand exposed at high water) during spells of hot dry summer weather the surface of the exposed beach has a very thin film of white salt crystals. That salt came from the previous spring tides that covered the beach (note that a spring tide has nothing to do with the season of spring, but indicates a very high tide). The saltwellers (those making salt) scraped up the top layer of sand with this salt. So little salt was gathered with the sand that huge amounts of sand had to be collected to make the venture profitable. In 1565, one sandweller at Hesketh Bank, for instance, is recorded as collecting about 500 large wagon-loads of salty sand.

The salty sand was piled into filters in the form of wooden or clay-lined stone troughs with holes in the bottom. Seawater was poured over the sand and, as the water percolated through, it dissolved the salt. The same salty water was used several times to dissolve the salt from several filter-loads of sand until its concentration was close to saturation point, and this point could be discerned because a fresh hen's egg will float in very concentrated brine.

The brine was taken away to the saltcoat (saltcote), or salt-house. There it was poured into lead vessels, a peat fire was lit underneath, and the water evaporated to leave damp salt crystals. This was put into baskets and allowed to dry thoroughly in the open air.

The increase of rock-salt mining in Cheshire in the eighteenth century made the laborious production of salt from seawater uneconomical and Lancashire's last saltcoat, at Hambleton by the Wyre estuary, closed in about 1780.

When I was a boy we and many other families bought blocks of rock salt. My mother would cut off chunks with the serrated-edged bread knife and I had the job of breaking this to salt grains on the kitchen table with the rolling pin. A couple of hours on a Saturday afternoon would produce enough salt to last the year. Today it is still possible to buy sea salt, produced in the Mediterranean, as well as finely ground rock salt. Years ago we used to put a few grains of dry rice in the saltcellar to prevent the salt absorbing water and 'caking'. Today, the anticaking agents magnesium oxide and sodium hexacy-anoferrate II are usually added to the salt, so we don't need to use the dry rice trick.

WATER, TEA, SUGAR AND ALE

Stocks Reservoir, high up on the fells east of Lancaster, was opened in 1930 to provide water for Blackpool.

COOKERY BOOKS RARELY TELL US MUCH ABOUT WATER, though water is an important ingredient of many recipes, is a cooking medium (as in boiled eggs or bain-marie cookery), and is the chief component of all drinks. Without water we die. Water constitutes about 85% of our body weight and 95% if our skeleton is ignored. Today we take tap water for granted and are wealthy enough to buy bottled water from the supermarket that costs 500 times more than tap water and is no better for us! How would we cope if, suddenly, an on-tap supply of clean water were no longer available? Our ancestors coped. Just.

When the population of Lancashire was almost entirely rural, drinking water was obtained from the then relatively unpolluted rivers and streams and from wells and springs. Some pollution by faecal bacteria must have occurred when several families or communities lived along river systems, for those upstream would contaminate the water reaching those downstream, and we know that diseases such as cholera, typhoid and dysentery were then endemic. However it seems quite likely that people living here two or three hundred years ago had a greater resistance to water-borne micro-organisms than we have today. Things changed from the middle of the eighteenth century when families quit the countryside for the towns and the urban populations of Lancashire exploded. Clean water then became a scarce commodity and deaths from water-borne diseases and from the inability to keep home and body clean became very common.

Manchester did have a public water supply as early as the 1560s, though the city then was little more than a large village. There was a spring on what is now King Street and the water from this spring was piped, using hollowed out tree trunks, to a building on Market Street. The building was locked at night and officials were on guard to keep out those collecting a bucket of water from polluting the supply. By the eighteenth century Mancunians obtained water from several other springs and wells, from the streams that join to make the Mersey, and by collecting rainwater flowing off roofs in butts. But, even when boiled, the water quality was poor. A report by Dr Thomas Percival noted that, in 1771, the people of Manchester were 'particularly subject to glandular obstructions and scrophulous swellings. Water loaded with stringent earthy salt has a direct tendency to produce such complaints.'

'THE PEOPLE OF MANCHESTER WERE "PARTICULARLY SUBJECT TO GLANDULAR OBSTRUCTIONS AND SCROPHULOUS SWELLINGS"'

Such supplies were completely inadequate once the population began to grow rapidly.

As Manchester's population began to grow (and the same applies to other towns in the county from Liverpool to Preston, Burnley and Blackburn) cheap buildings were hurriedly constructed to accommodate the newcomers. These were one-up-and-one-down back-to-backs or tenements built around a courtyard. These were not the type of terraced streets as shown in the introduction to *Coronation Street*, or that you can still see in every Lancashire town today. They had no back yards or even backdoors. They were literally back-to-back, where the back wall of one was back wall to the other. As these appalling pokey dwellings spread through the centres of our towns, those who could afford to moved out to more salubrious properties did so, and the larger houses in the town centres were then often let, room by room and cellar by cellar, to the poor families.

These homes had no indoor sanitation, no bathroom or kitchen, and not even an indoor water supply. There might be only one privy, usually draining into a cesspit but sometimes directly into a stream, shared between the occupants of twenty houses. In some parts of Liverpool there were two privies for sixteen houses, which might mean that upwards of a hundred people shared the same loo. Water usually came from standpipes or pumps in the squalid streets. One source, in Fountain Street, Manchester, was guarded to prevent people from polluting it by washing themselves or their clothes in its clean water. Open buckets were use to carry the water from the street into the dwelling. There would be enough for drinking and for cooking the simple meals that the poor folk ate, but there would not be enough to wash body, clothing or bedding regularly. In one particularly dreadful corner of Manchester, the middle of which is now occupied by Oxford Road railway station and then known as Little Ireland because of the concentration of Irish immigrants living there, each privy served at least 220 people. Frederick Engels described the scene there in his book *The Condition of the Working Classes in England* (1844): 'two hundred cottages … four thousand human beings … the cottages are cold, dirty, and of the smallest sort … streets uneven, fallen into ruts, and in part without drains or pavements; masses of refuse, offal and sickening filth lie among standing pools in all directions; the atmosphere is poisoned by the effluvia from these, and laden and darkened by the smoke of a dozen tall factory chimneys … the race that lives

'A VISIT TO CHAT MOSS' (*LEIGH JOURNAL*, 12 MAY 1893)

This article described the anonymous author's visit to Chat Moss, between Manchester and Warrington, during a long spring drought. At the time, piped water had reached only as far as Irlam, Tyldesley and Astley, and the farming families on the flat moss still relied on wells for their water.

'The remarkably dry Springtime of 1893, consisting in almost unprecedented sunny days of the past two or three months, has not injured or retarded the crops – at least on Chat Moss – but on the contrary it has proved beneficial to the cultivator, with one important exception … The drawback, the one serious source of discomfort and even danger on Chat Moss, is the absence of good water for man and beast. The wells, except in some few isolated instances, are empty, the miles of deep peat-sided ditches, ordinarily full of water, are most of them dry by reason of the long drought … One farmer made a big hole last year in which to wash celery before taking it to market. Some of this water, though foul and contaminated, remains and the owner and a few of his neighbours are obliged to use it, of course after filtering, for their domestic consumption. In other cases so scarce has this prime necessity of life become that when a person has had his daily ablution he sends the "soap suds" on to his next neighbour for further utilization in the same line, and ere the liquid substance is cast aside several persons have done their best to wash their hands and faces in it.'

This must have been a widespread problem throughout most of Lancashire in long periods of drought before the building of reservoirs.

in these ruinous cottages ... must really have reached the lowest stage of humanity.'

The consequence of such dreadful conditions faced by the majority of town and city dwellers was a higher than the average death rate. In 1841–50 the national death rate was 22 per 1000; in Manchester it was 33 and in Liverpool 36 per 1000. Epidemics of diseases like influenza and measles killed many who avoided typhus (a disease borne by the then common body louse), pulmonary tuberculosis (a bacterium transmitted in droplets in coughs and sneezes), and typhoid and cholera caught by drinking sewage-contaminated water. In 1846, in Liverpool, 53 per cent of children under the age of five years died. There were large outbreaks of cholera in 1836, 1849, 1854 and 1866. The 1849 epidemic coincided with a mass immigration from Ireland: it killed at least 5000 in Liverpool alone. A report on that epidemic to the General Board of Health described how, in Manchester, 'Innumerable privies ... [at] the back of long terrace ranges ... empty themselves into the filthy ditch [the River Medlock].' Then only 23 per cent of the 46,577 homes in Manchester had its own water supply, and that was turned off at night. Some 28 per cent had to go to collect their water from a standpipe in the street. The rest had no water supply at all, and had to collect what water they could from polluted wells and streams. It has been estimated that, in 1850, the population of Manchester needed about ten million gallons of water every day; the municipal water company could provide only three million gallons.

'INNUMERABLE PRIVIES ... [AT] THE BACK OF LONG TERRACE RANGES ... EMPTY THEMSELVES INTO THE FILTHY DITCH [RIVER MEDLOCK]'

Those latter statistics may seem dreadful, but only three decades earlier 88 per cent of Manchester households had to walk to gather their water in buckets.

Clearly something had to be done about housing, sewage treatment and water supply. In 1844 the old style of back-to-back slum was outlawed and regulations on the use of cellars for human habitation were introduced in 1853. Sewage schemes were introduced from the late 1840s which reduced the risk of contaminating the supply of drinking water. But there was no easy solution to the provision of clean water, for the water supplies within the growing towns were inadequate and certain to be contaminated with 'gut flora' and industrial effluents. Supplies would have to be piped in from the countryside. And, because Pennine rivers are spate rivers, running almost dry in summer droughts and in wasteful flood during winter rains, there would have to be storage. So reservoirs were built to gather river water that could be piped to town. The chain of reservoirs in Longdendale was built, at a cost of £1,167,428, to supply Manchester and Salford with 490 million gallons of water; the first water from these reached Manchester in 1857. But quickly demand exceeded supply, for not only were population and industry increasing (between 1847 and 1878 the number of customers seeking piped water in Manchester increased from 40,000 to 155,000) but as soon as tap water became available individual consumption increased. In 1832 water consumption for all purposes (drinking, washing, industrial etc) averaged 33 pints per person per day. By 1852 this had increased to 98 pints per day, in 1868 to 236 pints per day and in 1878 to 260 pints per day. Today, when the washing of clothes is a daily routine, when every day is a bath day, when the car needs washing on Sunday morning and the golf course needs irrigating, and when industries like brewing use a gallon of water to make a pint of beer, the average water consumption in Manchester is equivalent to a massive 665 pints per person per day.

'THE RACE THAT LIVES IN THESE RUINOUS COTTAGES … MUST REALLY HAVE REACHED THE LOWEST STAGE OF HUMANITY'

In 1894 the aqueduct from a deepened Thirlmere was completed to carry water the 96 miles from Cumbria to Manchester. By 1900 the City of Manchester was consuming 98 million gallons of water per day and demand was still growing. In 1920 that demand was satisfied by the piping of water from a deepened Haweswater.

Liverpool obtained its first Pennine water from the Anglezarke–Rivington complex of reservoirs, built in the hills above Chorley, in 1857. When this supply could no longer satisfy demand, Liverpool turned to the lakes of North Wales. Other developing towns in Lancashire built similar reservoirs by damming their nearest Pennine streams, sometimes constructing a series of dams so that, in wet periods, when one reservoir overflowed a reservoir downstream would catch the excess (for instance, Bolton has three reservoirs – Entwistle, Wayoh and Jumbles – on Bradshaw Brook to the northwest of the town). Sometimes surplus is piped down to lowland storage reservoirs: examples include the triple Audenshaw reservoirs just north of Denton and Heaton Park reservoir between Prestwich and Whitefield (Manchester), the Grimsargh reservoirs between Longridge and Preston, and Prescot reservoirs (Liverpool).

Water is still in small supply compared with demand, especially in drought-hit years. United Utilities, the company that now supplies Lancashire with its water, has to carry out a precarious balancing act in getting the water to where it is needed. It has also to face the politically difficult prospect of taking more water from the Lake District and North Wales that have a high rainfall, low human population, and are National Parks. We consumers should think on that every time we turn on the tap.

Do you take sugar in your tea?

Many of those evicted from the land by the eighteenth- and nineteenth-century Enclosure Acts 'attempted to find work in the growing towns and cities in the new factories being built. There, under the slavery of long hours and pittance wages, their diet declined to bread, jam, tea and sugar.'

Colin Spencer, *British Food*, 2000.

Tea was first brought to England by Catherine of Braganza, Queen to Charles II, in 1666. Like coffee, that reached these shores in about 1650, tea was at first very expensive and thus a drink for the wealthy. A large part of this expense was the tax imposed on its importation. In the eighteenth century the tax on dry tea-leaf was five shillings per pound and on liquid tea drunk in an inn or coffee house eight pence per gallon. Naturally, much tea was smuggled into England to evade this tax. Parson Woodforde described in his diary how, on the 29th March 1777, 'Andrews the smuggler brought me this night at about 11 o'clock a bagg of Hysons Tea 6 Pd [six pounds] weight. He frightened us a little by whistling under the Parlour window just as we were going to bed. I have him some Geneva [Holland gin] and paid him for the tea at 10/6 per Pd.'

Sugar, that gets its name from the Arabic *sukkar*, first reached England in 1205 from North Africa and later from Sicily. It too was very expensive and it remained the sweetener for the wealthy until the eighteenth century when cane sugar began to be imported from the North American and West Indian slave plantations. Suddenly refined white sugar became available at a relatively low cost and it quickly became one of the chief sources of carbohydrate for ordinary Lancastrians in cakes and puddings (see pages 132–145) and in tea. Some twentieth-century Lancashire housewives might have taken in as much as half their calorie intake as sugar in tea, while sweet strong tea became a worker's staple at tea breaks and mealtimes.

People started to put milk in their tea sometime in the nineteenth century, though many workers took sweetened black tea to work and were so used to black tea that, when they arrived home from work, their wives put only the tiniest amount of milk in the tea that they would drink with their evening meal.

Honey bees in their hive.

John Mackay
using smoke to
quieten a hive
of bees.

Honey

The only good sweetener of bygone days was honey, though unless you had your own hive, it would have been an expensive commodity, far beyond the pocket of most people, though occasionally a wild bee's nest might be found and its honey collected. Honey was also the essential ingredient in that medieval drink, mead.

John Mackay keeps his bees in the Lune valley and I visited him to gain an insight into this ancient occupation. We both donned beekeepers' suits and veils to avoid getting stung, but one did manage to pierce John's glove and give him a painful few minutes. He described how the hives work and the problems facing the beekeeper.

The hive consists of several wooden boxes, one on top of the other, though there are no tops or bottoms to the middle boxes so that bees can meander their way throughout the tower. The lower box is the brood nest. Here the queen lives and is prevented from moving to the upper layers by a queen excluder through which she cannot pass but the worker bees can. Here the queen's life is solely one of laying eggs and, in the peak period of June to August, she produces about 1500 per day.

The eggs are placed in wax cells and the larvae hatch and grow into worker bees in about 21 days. In summer the hive will contain upwards of 50,000 workers, each of which has a life span of about 33 days. For the first 19 days the workers remain in the hive as house bees, feeding larvae, building wax cells and generally tidying up the hive. Then they go to the entrance of the hive as guard bees before spending the rest of their lives flying out to gather pollen and nectar. They bring these back to the hive and lay down the honey in wax cells made on frames that the beekeeper puts in the boxes above the brood nest. As the honey accumulates another box, containing more frames, can be added to the hive.

Umpteen thousand journeys by worker bees are needed to produce one pound of honey so the most productive hives are those very close

to a source of pollen- and nectar-bearing flowers. Some beekeepers move their hives to take advantage of as many flushes of flowers as they can. For instance, in early spring the hives might be taken close to woodlands where snowdrops, bluebells and hazel are abundant. Then the hives may be taken to west Lancashire where oil-seed rape is widely grown (this produces a creamy, strong-tasting honey). And in late August the hives are taken to the heather moors and go on to produce some of the stickiest, sweetest of honeys.

There is a major problem when it comes to shifting hives around Lancashire. Bees will forage for a maximum of about three miles from their hive and they get to know this area very well. If you move a hive for two or three yards the bees that are out foraging can find their way back easily. Move it ten yards or a mile away, and the bees that are foraging cannot find their way to the hive. Instead they look where the hive was. However, if the hive is sealed with all the bees inside and moved more than three miles away into new territory the bees cannot relate to where the hive used to be and they learn the new position of the hive. So, if you want to move a hive just one mile, you must first move it about four miles away and let the bees get used to that position, and then you move it back three miles!

The ideal, John pointed out, is to keep the hives permanently in a place that is good for pollen and nectar throughout the year. And the best place in Lancashire for keeping bees? Skelmersdale!

One constant threat to the hive is a queen that dies, stops producing enough eggs or whose pheromones are failing. Then the workers react by putting eggs into especially large cells and feeding the larvae on a substance they make called royal jelly. Instead of producing a worker bee, the larva fed on royal jelly grows into a queen and, when she hatches, she will leave the hive, taking a large proportion of the workers with her. So the beekeeper must check every week that there are no unwanted queen cells in the hive, and be on the lookout in case a swarm of bees leaves the hive, though the swarm can often be collected and re-hived.

The worst part of beekeeping, John maintains, is extracting the honey, for it is a hot, sticky job that attracts wasps and bees and often results in getting stung. First of all the wax caps of the cells on the frames must be cut away. Then the frames are put in a centrifuge and the honey spun out of them. The honey must then be scraped from the centrifuge and filtered at least twice, to remove pollen grains, fragments of wax and bits of dead bee. In a good year a very productive hive might produce upwards of 100 pounds of cleared honey; in a poor year many hives will produce none.

So, if you have always thought that honey was expensive, you can see why!

Two salad dressings

Number One
4 tablespoons of good olive oil
4 tablespoons of walnut oil
4 tablespoons of white wine vinegar
2 tablespoons of honey
1 red chilli, finely chopped
1 clove garlic, well crushed

Number Two
6 tablespoons of olive oil
3 tablespoons of white wine vinegar
2 tablespoons of honey
2 tablespoons of French whole grain mustard

Put these in a jar, put on the lid and shake well before dressing a salad. Keep in the fridge and use within ten days.

Honey in the comb ... beautiful!

School Milk

Milk contains everything needed for a balanced diet except for vitamin C, iron and roughage. It was thus considered the ideal supplement to give to every schoolchild when, in the early 1930s, the government began to look to improving the heath of the nation's children. So in 1934 the Milk in Schools Scheme provided every schoolchild with a gill (one third of a pint) of milk every day.

I remember being given my small bottle of milk, with a straw, just before morning 'playtime' at Kirkham and Wesham junior school. Later, at Kirkham Grammar School, the milk for all 360 boys was piled in crates outside the door of the school canteen and we helped ourselves. On icy mornings we would thaw out the frozen milk on radiators before removing the silver foil top and, without straws, swig it down. Some boys did not like to drink milk, so some of us might devour two or even three bottles, often with a couple of slices of cold buttered toast, brought from home.

In 1939 the Milk Nutrition Committee found that twelve-year-old boys who had drunk school milk were three inches taller than their fathers had been at the same age, and claimed that those who drank school milk had quicker aptitude and were more intelligent than those who had not drunk their school milk.

Margaret Thatcher abolished school milk when she was Minister of Education in the Heath government of 1973 on the grounds that the diet of children had improved so greatly that they no longer needed the supplement. 'Thatcher the milk snatcher' later became one of Britain's longest-serving prime ministers.

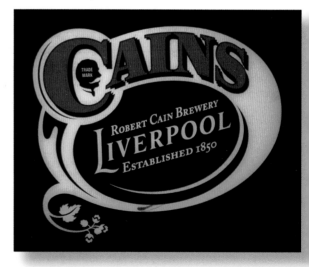

Cain's Ales of Liverpool. At one time Lancashire boasted scores of independent brewers; today few are left.

Writing a book about Lancashire's food is hard, thirsty work!

Ale and beer

Most of the alcoholic beverages drunk in Lancashire pubs up to the late 1970s were sorts of beer, not ale. For ale is not flavoured with hops; beer is. There were two sorts of ale. Small ale had a very low alcohol content and was used to quench thirsts without having any serious side-affects, whereas ale had a higher alcohol content that could easily lead to drunkenness.

The brewing of ale goes back to prehistory. It was part of the regular diet in medieval times, and monks were given a gallon of the stuff to drink every day. Was this light ale? Probably so. By 1500 the larger villages and towns had alehouses, where the traveller or those coming to market could join the local residents for refreshment. In about 1530 hops were introduced and the stronger-flavoured beer produced.

Through the twentieth century Lancashire had some of the finest brewers of bitter and mild beers, from Mitchell's of Lancaster, to Thwaites's of Blackburn, Higson's of Liverpool, Boddington's of Manchester, and with many in between them. Some, like the tiny independent brewer Fetler's of Rufford, are gone. Tetley, still a famous name in the world of beer, was once brewed in Leigh, but the brewery there has gone and the Tetley's mild and bitter sold in Lancashire pubs all now comes from the company's Yorkshire brewery.

Dedicated beer drinkers always shouted long and hard in favour of their own favourite brand (if given the choice I would always go for Thwaites). Some found the pub they liked best and would not go anywhere else for a drink. For years, ex-miner Bill Greg walked the best part of two miles to drink Tetley's bitter ('when it were brewed in Leigh, and not 'on t'other side o't Pennines') in the Nevison Inn on Plank Lane on the outskirts of Leigh, passing four other pubs on his way.

And there was a built-in routine in the drinking habits of the old keen beer drinkers. Ronnie Roberts also drank in the Nevison Inn. Every night he would arrive at ten minutes to ten, sit on a stool at the bar with the cheeks of his bum hanging over the edge, and take his first pint of Tetley's mild. All other customers had their pints in straight-sided glasses lacking handles. Not Ronnie. He drank his mild only from the squat, handled, tankard glasses. That was in the days of the 'Last orders', and 'Time up, gentlemen, please!' Ten to eleven was 'last orders', and by law everyone had to be gone by twenty past eleven. Most people ordered a pint or a half at last orders. Not Ronnie. 'Three pints!' he would say. As the three pints were being pulled and lined up in front of him on the bar he would quaff down the pint he was already holding and then hand the empty glass across the bar to Sheila, the landlady. 'Oh! And fill that one up as well!'

Ronnie Roberts was the life and soul of any party!

Anyone who can make half a gallon of beer disappear in fifteen minutes is not a drinker. He is a magician!

Alas, though drinking 'real ale' is popular in some circles, drinking the traditional Lancashire mild and bitter beers has declined greatly in favour of the chilled, higher alcohol foreign lagers that lack the richness and bite of a good bitter. Far worse, however, is the great decline in the number of real Lancashire pubs. They are losing out to the dreadful 'big-chain' pubs where cheap meals are served and TV and pop music prevent conversation.

Nettle Beer

One of the treats of going on a day trip to Heysham in the 1950s was a glass of nettle beer, bought from one of the fishermen's cottages in the old village. This had been brewed and allowed to ferment in the back kitchen, then poured from old cider bottles into half-pint glasses. It was three pence for a glass the last time I bought it in 1962.

'*CULPEPER'S HERBAL*: NETTLE BEER, "STAYETH BLEEDING OF THE MOUTH. IT IS GOOD FOR THE BITE OF A MAD DOG. IT IS GOOD FOR LETHARGY ..." '

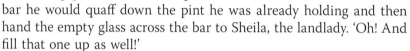

To make nettle beer, boil up some young nettle leaves, filter the brew and then add sugar, lemon juice and yeast. Let it ferment completely and then pour it into strong bottles. Before stoppering the bottles tightly, put in a pinch of sugar.

Get it right and you have a great drink. Get it wrong and the bottles will explode!

The Temperance Bar

Every town in Lancashire had its temperance bar where those who were fighting the demon drink could seek refuge with interesting non-alcoholic brews. Preston's temperance bar was on Lancaster Road, near the entrance of the old bus station. Like the old bus station, the temperance bar was demolished to make way for the Guild Hall.

As in real pubs, there was a bar at which you could sit or stand and talk with friends as you drank. At the back were huge ornate pot barrels, with a tap at the bottom, and with a label telling you what it contained. Real dandelion and burdock tasted far better than the fizzy stuff that masquerades as dandelion and burdock, and which contains neither dandelion nor burdock. One barrel held sarsaparilla, quite a tart drink that was highly recommended as a tonic for those who were 'run down'. Another barrel held diluted Vimto, a cordial that is still on sale here in Lancashire and one that has long been popular.

Come evening and a smoking, sooty little cart would appear and take up its place between the temperance bar and the bus station entrance. This sold 'baked' potatoes that were really semi-burnt potatoes with a crispy charcoal crust. With a lump of Stork margarine and a shaking of salt, for small boys, these were potato perfection!

Mawsons still produce authentic dandelion-and-burdock and sarsaparilla. Their stand at Southport Flower Show 2006.

Main Street, Heysham. A trip to Heysham was never complete without a glass of home-brewed nettle beer. Not so today. The Health & Safety brigade brought that Lancashire tradition to an end.

Sloe Gin

Sloes are the fruits of the blackthorn bush and, while the bushes are covered in shimmering white blossom every spring, in most years late frosts ruin the chance of a good crop of sloes in Lancashire, save for in sheltered spots by the coast. As an alternative, try damsons, though they do not produce quite as tart a drink.

Geoff Haslam is a specialist when it comes to making sloe gin. First of all he selects only the best juiciest sloes. He pricks these with a fork and then put them into a big glass jar. He adds sugar at the rate of eight ounces to a pound of sloes, adds a few drops of almond extract (some recipes add a dozen blanched almonds instead) and pours over this a 70cl bottle of the cheapest gin he can source. Geoff makes in bulk, most of us will be happy enough with a couple of bottles of the stuff!

Geoff Haslam and his special Bowland Sloe Gin.

Most people filter off the sloes just before Christmas and drink their sloe gin in the festive season. Geoff keeps his for a further twelve months, and it does improve with the keeping.

On a winter's day, out walking on the fells or by the sea, a nip of sloe gin is a welcome part of lunch. But beware, make it a single nip and no more.

What to do with the gin-soaked sloes? Remove all the flesh from the stones. Then get some plain ice cream and a basin. Fill the bowl with layers of ice cream and sloe flesh and put into the deep freeze. This tastes splendid with heavy Christmas pudding.

OATS AND WHEAT, PORRIDGE AND BREAD

'... blue milk [skimmed milk] and porridge were, for generations, the staple diet of the poorer worker.'
Edwin Waugh, in Joan Poulson, *Old Lancashire Recipes*, 1973.

Oats

UNTIL LAND DRAINAGE AND SOIL IMPROVEMENT occurred in lowland Lancashire and the lower Pennine slopes, the chief cereal grown in the county was oats. This is because oats are far more tolerant of cold, wet conditions than wheat, the other staple cereal that had provided those who lived in southern, eastern and central England with their bread from medieval times. Even now particularly wet summers can result in the loss of much of the wheat grown in Lancashire (as happened in 2004). So while today we are led to believe that rolled oats, oatmeal and porridge come from Scotland (and the porridge mined in the bogs of highland glens!) they are – or perhaps more accurately were – also Lancashire specialities. Only a few places in Lancashire were sufficiently well drained, usually on a south-facing slope, for growing wheat, and some of those places were given the name Wheatley (from wheat leigh, meaning wheat field), such as Wheatley Farm near Gisburn and Wheatley Lane in Pendle.

So until potatoes became an alternative to oats, oats was the main source of carbohydrate in the Lancastrian diet.

We can see this from the accounts recorded by Nicholas Blundell of Crosby for the second half of 1704. Blundell was a wealthy land-owner who ran a large household and during that six-month period he purchased 20 bushels of oats at one shilling (5p) per bushel, 30 bushels of potatoes at 7½ pence (3½ p) per bushel, and 5½ bushels of wheat at 4 shillings and 8 pence (23p) per bushel. Wheat, probably imported from further south in England, was an expensive luxury and in great demand among those who could afford to pay for it. The demand for wheat grew even greater when a milling technique was developed in 1872 that produced white, germless and bran-free flour. This produced a much softer, lighter bread than wholemeal, but one with many nutrients taken out. It is only in recent years that people have slowly turned back to the coarser but more flavoursome wholemeal and away from the glutinous white sliced loaf (that first appeared in shops in 1930).

Porridge

The easiest way of making oats digestible was to grind it into meal and turn the meal into porridge, which in some parts of Lancashire was known as *thick-thacks*. The basic recipe is:

> 1 pint water
> 2 oz fine oatmeal
> pinch salt

> Stir the oatmeal into the water, add the salt and bring to the boil, stirring all the time. Then simmer until the oatmeal is cooked. If using coarse oatmeal mix the ingredients in the pan and leave to soak overnight before boiling in the morning.

A slightly different method of making porridge, that added extra energy to the dish, was to melt some beef dripping in a pan and then to pour in boiling water. The oatmeal and salt were then stirred in, and the porridge allowed to simmer until the oats were cooked. This porridge, or gruel, would have been eaten as it was, though milk and/or honey may have been added. An alternative was called *dip-and-bore*, where a hole was made in a bowl of thick porridge which was then filled with syrup, treacle or honey.

A thicker, grittier porridge was known as Hasty Pudding. 8 oz of oatmeal and a pinch of salt was stirred into a pint of cold water.

The pan was then brought to the boil and then simmered for only four minutes, stirring constantly. If available, butter or suet, sugar or honey, and cream or milk might be added before eating.

Another Lancashire variant of porridge was known as *waff*. This was porridge made with water as described earlier, but before being served a liberal helping of treacle was stirred in and milk was poured over the dish before eating.

Porridge was, and still is, eaten hot and makes a warm, filling breakfast cereal without the additives found in many industrially produced packet-cereals. Today 'rolled oats' are most often seen in the supermarkets. These result in porridge with a very creamy consistency. For the real connoisseur, however, the best porridge is still made from pure and unadulterated oatmeal.

Oat breads

Oatmeal has long been used to prepare simple breads. In Lancashire there were two sorts of oat bread, clapbread and riddlebread (also called oatcake). Both are very simple to make once the basic techniques have been mastered.

Clapbread

In her book *Through England on a Side-Saddle* (1695) Celia Fiennes described how, when she crossed the River Wyre and arrived at Garstang, she was 'first presented with the clap bread which is much talked of, made all of oats'.

> Make a stiff dough by adding a little water to a bowl of oatmeal to which a couple of pinches of salt have already been mixed. Put the dough on a board and flatten by striking it with the hands until is an even half an inch thick; it is this action that gives clapbread its name. Cook the clapbread on an iron bakestone (also called in Lancashire a bakstone and backstone), turning it to ensure both sides are crisp and lightly browned; you can also use a heavy iron frying pan. Clap bread is an excellent alternative to biscuits to go with good Lancashire cheese.

> *Throdkin* was a variation on clapbread, in which a little finely chopped salted pork belly or side (see page 68) was mixed with the oat meal to add extra flavour.

Riddlebread (or Lancashire Oatcake or Browse)

Professor Gordon Manley was raised and educated in Blackburn before heading south to Cambridge University. There he became Britain's greatest climatologist, and is still famed for his back-calculation of the English climate for every year back to the middle of the seventeenth century, and for his great book, *Climate and the British Scene.* In the mid 1960s he spent a few years establishing the Department of Environmental Studies at the new Lancaster University and that was where I met him.

'The little store in Pilling?' he asked. 'Does it still sell Lancashire oatcake?'

It did; but it does not now.

'OATMEAL HAS LONG BEEN USED TO PREPARE SIMPLE BREADS'

> Add a quarter of a pint of boiling water to half a pint of semi-skimmed milk. Then add two pounds of fine oatmeal, half an ounce of yeast, a pinch of bicarbonate of soda and a little salt. If you cannot obtain fresh yeast, dissolve a teaspoon of dry yeast in a little tepid water and add that to the mix instead. Stir well and leave covered in a warm place for half an hour. The result should be a batter with a pouring consistency. If not, then add either more oatmeal (if too runny) or tepid water (if too stiff).

> Pour a ladleful of batter onto an iron bakstone (again you can use a large heavy frying pan) and smooth to a constant thickness of about one eighth of an inch. This used to be done with a scraper made of hardwood called a back-spittle; today a kitchen spatula might be used. Cook until the underside is brown and the upper side soft but set. When removed from the bakstone the riddlebread is smooth on the cooked side, rough on the other side and looks rather like an oval piece of chamois-leather.

Riddlebreads were hung over a special wooden frame called a bread-flake (rather like a small clothes horse or, as we call them in Lancashire, a clothes-maiden) to cool and dry out before being stored or sold in the shop. Sometimes they were eaten before being dried, in which case they were sometimes called *soft cake*; after being dried on the bread-flake they were sometimes called *soap and rattle*. They were a common sight in bakers' and grocers' shops and on the markets up to the late 1960s. Buttered, they are excellent with jams or marmalade, rolled up with savoury fillings, or used to mop up gravy with meat dishes (oatcake soaked with gravy was known as *brewis*). Someone eating a stew with oatcake was said to be enjoying *stew and hard*, and when a damp oatcake was sprinkled liberally with salt it was then a *salty cat*.

Riddlebread is probably the most ancient of breads in Britain for there is evidence that a simple recipe was used in Bronze and Iron Age times up to 4000 years ago. Then oatmeal was finely ground with a quern and added to water to make a thick porridge. Salt may have been added, though in these prehistoric times salt was a very scarce commodity other than for people living close to the coast. A small quantity of this porridge was poured on a hot bakstone over an open fire.

Oatmeal Bread

Neither clapbread nor riddlebread resemble bread as we know it today, made from wheat flour and yeast. Oatmeal bread is more 'bread-like' because wheat flour and yeast are used in the recipe.

Gluten is an elastic protein, found in flour, which is stretched by the carbon dioxide bubbles produced by yeast as the bread 'rises'. When the bread is then baked the oven's heat fixes the stretched gluten so that the loaf permanently has the spaces in it formed by the carbon dioxide bubbles.

Oat, rye and barley flours have less gluten than wheat, so bread made from them tends to be hard and more compact than bread made with wheat. However, different varieties of wheat have different amounts of gluten. Durum wheat has the most gluten and is used to make pastas and spaghetti; the gluten helps these hold their shape when boiled in water for several minutes. At the other extreme are wheat flours with much less gluten and we use them when making cakes and puddings; there is enough gluten to hold shape but not enough to make the cake or pudding heavy or chewy. Bread flour comes in between the two extremes, and though it is often labelled as 'strong' flour, it is not as strong as flour made from durum wheat.

While bread made from wheat flour was introduced to Lancashire from the major wheat-growing regions of England and is now by far the commonest bread produced, there is one bread recipe, oat bread, devised in Lancashire that retains the traditional oat but exploits the gluten of wheat.

Soak 8 oz of fine oatmeal in half a pint of milk for about one hour.

Dissolve one teaspoon of sugar in 2 fl.oz of warm water and mix in three teaspoons of dried yeast (or one ounce of fresh yeast). Leave for 10–15 minutes until frothy.

Put the soaked oatmeal, ¾ lb strong white (bread) flour, ½ teaspoon salt and 1 oz melted lard or butter in a warm bowl and mix. Add the liquid yeast and then mix thoroughly to a dough and kneed to a ball. Cover with a cloth and put in a warm place until it has risen to twice its original size.

Knead again for two minutes before cutting the dough in two equal pieces, and form each into a round cob shape. Cover with a cloth and put back in a warm place until they have doubled in size.

Brush top of each cob with milk and sprinkle over a little oatmeal.

Bake for about 25 minutes in a very hot oven.

Note: this bread can be flavoured with black treacle (add about one tablespoonful to the above mix), and then it is known as *jannock*.

Oatmeal and Ginger Jannock

A recipe from the Leigh-Wigan area from about 1910 added ginger to the treacle-flavoured oatcake.

Mix half a pound of plain flour, quarter of a pound of oatmeal, three ounces each of sugar and butter, a tablespoonful of black treacle and a teaspoonful each of powdered ginger and baking powder. Add milk and make into a stiff dough. Bake in a moderate oven for 1½ hours.

Oatmeal Cake

This simple recipe was found in an old note book belonging to a long-gone great aunt of Elizabeth Davies, who lived in the Wigan area, and dates from about the end of the nineteenth or beginning of the twentieth century. It is interesting to note that nearly all the recipes are of puddings and cakes (some appear on pages 132–145), and that only one is savoury (a salmon paste, page 113).

Mix four tablespoons of oatmeal with four tablespoons of flour, three tablespoons of sugar, a teaspoon of baking powder, one egg and a quarter pound of butter. Make into a stiff dough using a little milk. Mould into small flat cakes and fry on both sides until brown and crisp.

Scrapple

This is an interesting and probably very old dish based on the two staples, oatmeal and pork. One modern version suggests using very lean pork, but a hundred years and more ago the vogue was for as much fat as possible. It is also likely that salt pork, the meat that kept the family going through the long winter months, was used in scrapple.

Take about three pounds of pork, cut into small pieces, some pork bones (e.g. ribs, shoulder blades) and a large chopped onion, and put in a large pan of water. Bring to the boil and simmer until the meat is very tender. This may be only an hour or so if lean pork is used, but up to three hours if a tougher cut is used. Sieve the stock produced into a clean pan, discard the bones (that will have added flavour and some gelatine to the stock) and chop very finely, or mince, the cooked meat. Put the meat back into the stock, bring to the boil and add one pound of medium oatmeal, and salt and pepper to taste. Slowly simmer for one hour. Pour the hot scrapple into greased moulds (bread tins are ideal) and put in a cool place to set. To serve, slice and fry until brown on both sides.

Great with black pudding and Lancashire sauce!

Other uses of oatmeal

Oatmeal mixed with water was often used to thicken stews, just as today we might use flour and water or Bisto. Oatmeal and water mixed for this purpose was known as *lire*.

Fine oatmeal was often fried in bacon fat and eaten warm. This simple dish was known as *pomdoaf* and *stirabout*.

Oatmeal is of course an essential ingredient of parkin (page 138).

Wheat bread

Wheat flour and cakes and bread made with wheat flour almost eliminated oats from the Lancashire diet during the late nineteenth and early twentieth century, although wheat flour bread arrived in the county after most of the rest of England.

Lancastrians have several names for small white bread 'rolls'. They may be called: barm cakes, flour cakes, plain teacakes, oven-bottom cakes, muffins, baps, rolls and, less commonly, pikelins, pickelins, bunnocks and cobs.

Bacon Shapes

From the 1930s up to the present day, the most popular sort of white bread has been the soft white sliced loaf made by companies such as Mother's Pride and Rathbones. It was the basis of the jam butty and bacon butty. In poorer households, however, not everyone could have bacon on their bacon butties, so from Higher Ince, near Wigan, came the bacon shape.

Take a slice of bacon and fry it gently in lard for a minute or so. Lift the bacon, dripping with fat, and place it across a slice of Mother's Pride. Put another slice of bread on top, and press the two slices together. Now peel apart the two slices of bread and remove the bacon. Give the slices of fatty bread, with the imprint of the shape and a whiff of flavour of the bacon, to the children. The bacon can be returned to the frying pan with more lard and a second set of bacon shapes made with two more slices of bread. A third set of bacon shapes can then be made before, finally, the cooked crispy bacon is made into a bacon butty for father.

What the Lancashire coalminers took down t'pit.

Some Lancashire miners called the food that they ate underground 'jack-bit' and others 'snap'. The origin of the first is unclear, but 'snap' comes from the tin box in which they carried their food.

It has been said that the food carried by the miners was a sort of pasty called 'Lancashire Foots' (see page 49). The story goes that the Lancashire foots was designed to fit into a snap-tin. That Lancashire foots is a county food and an excellent pasty there is no doubt. However it seems that most miners carried far simpler fare. Bread-and-dripping or jam butties were most popular. (Incidentally, a jam butty in Lancashire was sometimes called a *jarvy buttie*.) One Leigh miner put it this way: 'Down t'pit tha' couldn't taste owt. Jam didn't taste like jam down theer!'

Alas, the Lancashire coalmining industry is no more. Yet in these days of the talk of an energy crisis, it is galling to think that there is more coal still underneath Lancashire than was ever brought up to the surface.

Bread and milk

Bread soaked in milk became a very popular dish in Lancashire during the first half of the twentieth century. It was known as *pobs* or, more locally in the county, *babsops*, and in its most basic form it was a useful way of using up stale white bread. Children grew to like it, especially when warm milk was used and the pobs sweetened with sugar. Peter Unsworth, who was raised in Oldham, said that it was 'delicious!'

John Hesketh was brought up near Burscough in the 1940s and 1950s and he had a form of pobs called *tay pottick* every morning before setting out to school. White bread was put in a bowl and it

'THERE WAS ALWAYS A HOT POT OF TEA ON THE STOVE

was soaked with hot tea from the tea-pot ('There was always a hot pot of tea on the stove', he said). Then tinned condensed milk was poured over it. Some of John's schoolmates also had tay pottick for their breakfasts, and some of them sprinkled sugar over the top before adding the condensed milk.

And what are Peter and John's reactions now to their childhood bread-and-milk dishes? Peter's wife had to go into hospital for a few days, and as a special treat Peter made up some pobs for his children. 'They refused to eat it!' he protested. 'But then I tried it. It was horrible!'

John too has tried his old breakfast dish recently. He grimaced when asked what he thought of it now.

Pikelets

Some Lancastrians call crumpets pikelets, but the true Lancashire pikelet is something different and, in contrast to the last dish, delicious. They are more akin to drop scones or so-called scotch pancakes.

Take half a pound of plain flour and half a pint of either skimmed milk or a 50:50 mix of full cream milk and water, and mix well (a food processor now makes making pikelet batter a minute's job). Add a large egg and whisk in. Add a heaped dessertspoon of caster sugar and half a teaspoon of salt, and mix. Finally add 2½ teaspoonfuls of baking powder, and mix well in.

Fry in a well-greased frying pan, making each pikelet from two good tablespoons of batter (my mother's frying pan could fry five at once), until they are brown on each side. My two brothers and I used to eat them warm, buttered with strawberry jam, faster than my mother could fry them! Fifty years later and this comforting flavour of Lancashire seems to have almost vanished!

POTATOES

'The weavers were labouring under the most incredible privation; they did not earn a sufficiency to procure them meat, except occasionally, or more frequently once a week. Their ordinary food was oatmeal and potatoes, mutton broth, gruel, mutton dripping on stale bread, water and beer ... a family of 12 ate only gruel twice a day, potatoes once and herrings [salted, see page 110] sometimes ... the pan they used was borrowed.'

James Clegg, *A Chronological History of Bolton*, 1800.

POTATOES, COMMONLY CALLED PRAYTERS in the county, were first grown commercially in Lancashire at Formby in the 1670s. By 1680 a toll was imposed on carts carrying potatoes from the flatlands of southwest Lancashire to Wigan market. By about 1700 potatoes were also being grown around Garstang where, the food historian Colin Spencer suggests, lobscouse was invented (Liverpudlians please note! see page 48).

The great increase in the production of potatoes in Lancashire was driven by two factors: the first was the tremendous increase of the poor urban population who needed basic foodstuffs to fill their empty bellies, and the second was that potatoes, being easily carried packets of starch, were ideal for the job. But to produce potatoes cheaply, close to the centres of the exploding human population, needed lots of extra land. This land was won from the vast peaty mosslands in the south and west of the county.

The land on either side of the Mersey between Manchester and

Warrington, and across the west Lancashire plain between Liverpool and Preston, and between Ribble estuary and Morecambe Bay, is dominated by mosslands. In their natural state mosslands are huge tracts of fenland, bog, heather moor and birch scrub with, in several places, shallow lakes (Martin Mere inland of Southport was finally drained in the 19th century, and Marton Mere inland of Blackpool remains). As demand for food grew, so it became profitable to drain the mosslands, burn off the natural vegetation, and to plough them. The mossland soil consisted of pure peat up to thirty feet deep (37 feet in parts of Chat Moss, just to the west of Manchester), so it held little in the way of plant nutrients and it was very acidic. So the land was heavily limed or marled at a rate of 150–160 tons per acre and then manure was spread over it. In the mosslands close to Manchester and Liverpool human manure, called 'nightsoil', was used; in the early 1840s 20,000 tons were being used every year to enrich the parts of Chat Moss that had been reclaimed. It is still possible to find traces of this nightsoil on ploughed mossland fields in the form of bits of broken pottery and glass that had been thrown onto the muckheap.

‘ IN 1847, 21,482 TONS OF DRY GUANO (BIRD DROPPINGS) REACHED LIVERPOOL, DESTINED FOR THE ARABLE LANDS OF WEST LANCASHIRE ’

Further north, in the Pilling and Cockerham area, farmyard manure was mixed with guano (dried seabird droppings) imported from Peru through Liverpool and carried north via the Rufford branch of the Leeds and Liverpool canal and then the Lancaster canal. In one year (1847) 21,482 tons of dry guano reached Liverpool, most of it destined for the newly reclaimed arable lands of west Lancashire.

A detailed report, *Farming in Lancashire*, published in 1849 stated that, 'The moss-land is found to produce the best potatoes of any known; and whilst in other soils the failure of this crop has been a total or partial loss to the cultivator, the moss-farmer is reaping an abundant harvest. On the customary Lancashire acre he can get:

	£.	s.	d.
60 loads of large potatoes, at 10s	30	0	0
20 loads of small potatoes, at 7s	7	0	0
	£37	0	0'

One load weighed 240 lbs (109kg).
The same report estimated that it cost about fifteen shillings (75p) to convert an acre of worthless mossland into rich arable land, and that its rent every year would be worth over one pound to the landowner who had carried out the reclamation.

Of course, reclaimed mossland was not used to grow only potatoes. To avoid a build-up of pests and disease crop rotation was practised, and the rotation on Lancashire mosslands included (and still includes) carrots, turnips and beetroot, leeks and onions, sprouts, cabbages and cauliflowers, and oats, barley and wheat. Thus was grown, within easy carriage distance, all the basic vegetables needed to feed the growing urban population of Lancashire.

Most potatoes were boiled, probably in their skins, which were peeled away just before they were eaten. In the poorest families, besides salt, a little melted dripping or lard would be the only accompaniment. However there were, and still are, some appetizing ways in which Lancashire cooks could prepare dishes dominated by the humble potato.

What our Lancashire mosslands looked like before being drained and turned into farmland. Deep, saturated peat that supported a wonderful array of wild flowers, like the yellow bog asphodel (often also called the Lancashire asphodel).

Potato Cakes

Many shop-bought potato cakes are heavy, stodgy, with too much flour and not enough potato, but there are many recipes for good home-made versions.

The simplest goes as follows: take well mashed boiled potatoes, add salt and butter to taste, mould into round, half-inch thick cakes, and fry on a hot griddle (or frying pan). These are great with a cooked bacon-and-egg breakfast.

Alternatively, mash one pound of boiled potatoes with a tablespoon of milk. Then mix in 4 oz plain flour, 2 oz melted butter and salt to taste. Finally mix in one beaten egg. Fry on a hot griddle (or frying pan) or bake in a moderate oven until brown.

This richer potato cake may have chopped spring onion (or ordinary onion), a few herbs such as thyme and parsley, and some good grated Lancashire cheese added.

Potato Scallops

Peel and slice 2 lbs of potatoes and one large onion. Take two rashers of bacon and chop them into tiny pieces. Grease a dish and layer the potato and onion, scattering the bacon bits through. Add water to within half an inch of the top of the last layer, which should be potato. Put a lid on the dish and cook in a moderate oven for about 1½ hours; take the lid off for the last 20 minutes so that the top layer of potatoes becomes a nice brown colour.

These may be eaten as they are. However, a small helping will make a tasty potato dish to go with things like baked or fried trout (use smoked bacon) or roast chicken.

Lancashire Hot Pot

If there is one thing that gets Lancastrian cooks arguing it is how to prepare an authentic Lancashire hot pot. Go to Preston and Blackburn and the hot pot usually contains carrots, but go to Bolton and Leigh and it does not. I have known people put swede into their hot pot, some mushrooms (though the only mushrooms available when the dish was invented were field mushrooms and then only in late summer). Others have used beef instead of lamb. I have witnessed tattie-hash (page 46) with a suet crust on top being served as hot pot, and there are even some who have put curry powder in their hot pots. I suppose you can put in your hot pot anything you like. But don't call it a Lancashire hot pot!

First of all, the hot pot is named after the pot in which it is cooked. This was traditionally brown, glazed earthenware, with a lid that had two small holes through which steam could escape.

The second point is that real Lancashire hot pot was a peasant dish, based on potato, flavoured with onion and the cheapest cut of mutton or lamb, and with water as the cooking liquid (NOT dissolved Oxo or stock cube!). If you were feeling a bit better off one week you might add one or two extra ingredients – perhaps a chopped carrot or a sliced kidney. Properly made, such a simple hot pot is an inexpensive, nutritious, warming comfort dish. As soon as you start to make the hot pot more elaborate, by adding things like oysters or fillet of lamb, it may be a very good dish to eat, but it ceases to be a traditional hot pot.

Note that many modern recipes rightly have the ingredients layered, including the meat. Traditionally, however, there was not enough meat to form layers (it would be one, not two or three chops per person), so the meat was placed in one layer, just below the top layer of potatoes so that the flavour would percolate down through the whole dish.

A basic hot pot to serve six:

> "IT WAS NOTED IN 1833 THAT A FEW POTATOES AND HALF A POUND OF MUTTON FAT HAD PROVIDED FIVE DINNERS FOR A FAMILY OF FIVE IN BURNLEY."
> ALAN CROSBY, *A HISTORY OF LANCASHIRE*, 1998

Slice 2½lbs peeled potatoes and two large peeled onions. Put a layer of potatoes, then onion, then potatoes, then onion and so on until you have only enough potatoes left to make the top layer. Add seasoning at this stage (salt and pepper to taste). Now place six scrag-end of neck lamb or mutton chops on top. You may like to use better quality chops, and in these days of worry about eating animal fat you may like to trim away most of the fat, though when the hot pot was invented people needed as much energy from their food as they could obtain and fat does add flavour. Cover the lamb with the last layer of potatoes. Pour water into the hot pot so that it reaches the top of the lamb. Put on the lid and cook in a slow oven for 2–2½ hours. Remove the lid and cook for a further 30 minutes to brown and crisp up the top layer of potatoes.

Serve with pickled beetroot or red cabbage.

Note: If you want to add swede, turnip or carrot to your hot pot, then add those as a separate layer in the middle of the dish.

Tattie-hash (pronounced 'tay-ta ash')

This was one quick way of providing nourishing food with the minimum of cost, the meat being leftovers from the Sunday roast (lamb or beef or pot-roast beef).

The ingredients are (to serve six): 2½ lbs peeled and chopped potatoes, 2 large onions peeled and chopped, 2 large carrots sliced, leftover meat, very finely chopped. Put everything into a large pan, season with salt and pepper, and pour in enough beef stock to cover. Bring to the boil and then simmer for about 40 minutes with a pan lid on. Then remove the pan lid and continue to simmer for a further 20 minutes. The idea is to get the vegetables very soft and then to evaporate off water so that the hash thickens without the use of corn flour or Bisto!

Corned beef hash is made in exactly the same way using a tin of corned beef cut into cubes.

MEAT AND POTATO PIE

Meat and potato pie has long been a traditional party fare among Lancastrian communities, but the following event, described by Mrs Jean Searle (née Hartley) must have been a party to remember.

Harry and Doris Hartley were landlord and landlady of the Toll Bar Inn at Horwich but preparing to retire to Blackpool. They decided that their farewell would consist of meat and potato pie, but the problem was how to make a meat and potato pie for all their 150-plus customers. This was in 1959, when most families still had a big boiler and not a washing machine for washing clothes on Washday Monday, so it was decided to make the pie in that.

Soon after dawn on the day before their departure the family were up and peeling a hundredweight sack of potatoes and bags of carrots and onions. A pile of beef was cut up into small pieces. Water, salt and pepper, and Oxo cubes and gravy browning were added to the boiler full of food. Then Harry lit the gas and soon the cauldron began to make a 'glug, glug, glug sound. I can still remember that it smelt gorgeous,' said Jean.

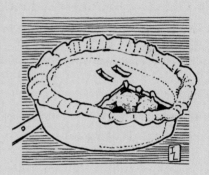

She continued, 'Then we laid out dishes of pickled red cabbage, beetroot and onions all along the bar, and mum and grandma baked lots of pastry crusts in the oven. When we came to serve the pie we put a square of crust on top of each dish of the meat and potato pie mix. Everyone enjoyed it. I often think, when I push the button on my automatic washing machine, that I couldn't cook a meat and potato pie in there!'

And Jean finished her narrative with a contentious point. 'I also think that, for a party like that one, meat and potato pie would beat hot pot any day.'

Meat and Potato Pie, with a suet crust

There was a cafuffle a few years ago when the Trades' Description people objected to the term 'meat and potato pie' when the commercially produced pie contained a minute amount of meat. Instead, professional bakers had to call their wares potato and meat pies. I suppose the Nanny State people were technically correct ... but the Lancashire meat and potato pie *is* a potato pie to which a little meat has been added to give flavour.

The pies my grandfather took to the mill were completely enclosed in pastry, as are the commercially produced pies. This pie, to cook and eat at home, has a suet crust only on the top.

The ingredients are: 1 lb finely chopped or coarsely minced lean beef (e.g. braising steak), 2 lbs peeled and cubed potatoes, 1 large onion chopped, 2 large carrots chopped and 1½ pints of beef stock.

Put these into a large pan, season with salt and pepper, bring to the boil and simmer for a good hour. Using a slotted spoon, put the cooked ingredients into a dish with a little of the cooking liquid. Then put a suet crust lid over and cook in a moderate oven for about 45 minutes.

Served with pickles, this is a great dish to serve when family members gather at midnight to greet the New Year. It helps soak up the various beverages that may have been consumed earlier in the evening!

Lobscouse

Earlier I noted that this dish might have been invented at Garstang, though another (anonymous) food historian suggested North Wales. Whatever. The name first appeared in print in 1706 in an obscure little book about the Royal Navy by E.Ward, called *Wooden World Dissected*: 'He has sent the fellow to the Devil, that first invented Lobscouse.'

Because it is so easy to make (it is really a form of tattie-hash) it became a popular dish in ships' galleys. The sailors of Liverpool took to eating a lot of lobscouse … and we know the rest. Lobscouse, lobby, or scouse is not always cooked with meat. When it isn't it is called 'blind scouse'. In the early days it is likely that blind scouse was eaten more often than full scouse.

Like hot pot, scouse is a collection of what ingredients one can beg, borrow or steal. One recipe includes dried peas, but I have never eaten a scouse in Liverpool containing peas. The absolute and essential ingredients are potatoes and onions.

> 'HE HAS SENT THE FELLOW TO THE DEVIL, THAT FIRST INVENTED LOBSCOUSE'

To feed ten hungry mouths you need, peeled and chopped: 5–6 large potatoes, 2 large or 3 small onions, 1 small or ½ a large swede, 4–5 carrots, 1 leek, 2 lbs of good stewing steak or silverside cut into diced, mixed herbs, a tablespoon of dripping (or oil), salt and pepper and at least one pint of beef stock.

Brown the meat in dripping or oil in a large pan. Add stock, herbs and seasoning and bring to the boil before simmering for 2–2½ hours. Now add all the vegetables and simmer for 1½ hours, topping the pan up with stock or water if tending to get too dry.

With this sort of stew, the flavour and texture seems to be enhanced if it is made the day before and then warmed up just before it is eaten.

Serve in bowls with chunks of good wholemeal bread.

Bolton Meat Pie

This variation on the theme of potato, onion, carrot and meat was made in large volumes in a pub in Bolton, now long gone. In the old days, when men gathered at Saturday lunchtime, having spent the morning working in the cotton mill, they would have a helping of this hefty dish with a few pints of mild before heading to Burnden Park to watch Nat Lofthouse and the Wanderers kick off at 3pm.

> Line a big casserole with lamb chops and put over them a layer of sliced Bury black pudding. Over that layer sliced potato, carrot and onion, using the last layer of potatoes to fill the dish. Add seasoning after each triple layer. Pour in lamb stock (use good stock cubes) until its level reaches the top of the potatoes. Cover and put the dish in a slow oven for 4–5 hours, then remove the lid and cook for another half hour in a moderate oven.

Lancashire Foots

This dish is said to have been a pasty specially made to fit into the miner's snap-tin (see page 15). However, most Lancashire miners seem to have taken a simpler fare down the pit. Nevertheless, this is the Lancashire equivalent of the Cornish pasty, and is equally authentic. Alas, commercial bakers in the county insist on selling us the Cornish version, and not our own!

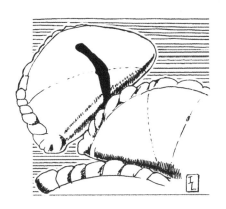

> To make a pair of Lancashire foots:
>
> Take ¾lb skirt beef, a chopped onion, 1½lbs peeled and chopped potatoes and ½ pint beef stock and cook in a dish in a slow oven for two hours. Then let is cool.
>
> Take a pound of short crust pastry and roll it into a large oval. Cut this oval longitudinally into two halves. Take each half and roll one end out to give a foot-shaped piece of pastry with a foot and a narrower heel.

Using a slotted spoon, take the cooked meat and vegetable mix and pile it on each of the heels. Then wet the edge of the heel and pull the sole over to form the pasty. Press down the edges to seal. Place each foot on a greased baking tray, brush with beaten egg, and cook in a moderate oven for 25–30 minutes, until the pastry is cooked and brown.

Lancashire foots are excellent for picnics. If you want variety then as alternative fillings try:

1. Cheese and onion: use grated good Lancashire cheese and raw onion.

2. Chicken and mushroom: use the leftovers of a roast chicken, with chopped raw mushroom, moistened with a little seasoned cream.

Like any sort of pasty, you can make up your own filling. Banana and smoked bacon?

‘A CURE FOR TONSILITIS USED IN THE DEANE AREA OF BOLTON IN THE 1930S: BOIL AND THEN SLICE A LARGE POTATO AND THEN BIND TO THE THROAT WITH A FLANNEL BANDAGE ’

VEGETABLES

COOKED VEGETABLES AS WE KNOW THEM TODAY in 'meat and two veg.' dinners are a fairly modern and universal part of meals. In the old days, wealthier folk ate lots of meat and the minimum of vegetables, whereas the poor who could afford little meat would eat what vegetable material they could, cooked in a stew or soup.

From Anglo-Saxon times rural Lancastrians grew much of their plant foods, including onions, leeks, garlic, peas, beans, carrots, swedes, turnips and cabbages. A nourishing daily meal, or *potage*, could be produced from these in a cauldron suspended over an open fire. If available, a few scraps of bacon or salt pork might be added to give extra flavour. It is only a small step – that of adding more water, plus seasoning and a few herbs – to making vegetable soup, and to this day vegetable soups are one of the great flavours of Lancashire.

The basic vegetable soup is:

¾ lb mixed vegetables, finely chopped, to four pints of stock
or,
1 lb mixed vegetables, finely chopped, to four pints of water.

Simmer in a large pan until all the vegetables are cooked!

Onion is the only essential ingredient in such a primitive soup, and carrot, turnip, swede, cabbage, sprout, cauliflower, leek, garlic, tomato, peas and beans, potato and more 'exotic' vegetables such as sweet corn, squash, sweet potato and kohlrabi, might be included. So too might a tablespoon of pearl barley and/or lentils. Such soups were often thickened by adding a thick slice of stale bread. The French peasants took this one stage further by toasting the bread with cheese on the top or deep-frying the bread to produce croutons. We might do the same: simply make cheese-on-toast and float that on your soup.

Lancashire's Robinsons of Forton produce the best seed if you want to grow huge vegetables. You can see what is possible if you visit their stand at Southport Flower Show.

Pea Soup

In winter pea soup was very popular in Lancashire because it used one of the great staples of the medieval household, the dried pea. It is very easy to make:

> Fry a small onion and a carrot, finely chopped, in butter, stirring all the while until they are brown. Add four pints of water and bring to the boil. Add half a pound of dry split peas and simmer for three hours. Cooking time will be reduced if the peas are soaked in cold water overnight. Before serving add a dessert spoon of brown sugar and salt and pepper to taste.

Pea and Ham Soup

This is an old Lancashire favourite.

Soak one pound of dried peas in plenty of cold water overnight. Take either a ham shank or some bacon ribs and if they are thought to be excessively salty soak them in water overnight.

Boil the ham shank or bacon ribs in water until the meat is very tender. Remove the shank or ribs, but retain the stock. Take all the meat from the bones and chop it into tiny bits.

Put the soaked peas into the stock, bring to the boil and simmer for about one hour. Then add the meat and a couple of finely chopped carrots. Bring back to the boil and simmer until the peas are mushy.

Some people put in some suet dumplings for the last 20–30 minutes to add bulk to the soup.

Potato and Leek Soup

Wild pink-footed geese from Iceland are very fond of potatoes and carrots.

This was a very popular soup in the late eighteenth and early nineteenth century among those who lived on the mosslands of west Lancashire.

A peasant dish? Well try this. Let the soup cool and then blitz it in the food processor. Put it is the fridge to get it well chilled; putting the soup in the freezer gets it even cooler. Serve, ice cold, with freshly ground black pepper and in the centre of each bowl pour a couple of tablespoons of cream. Delicious of a hot summer's day. The French gave this peasant soup a posh name: vichyssoise.

Boiled Onions

A large, peeled onion, gently boiled until it is nice and soft, served with butter, salt and white pepper was a very popular snack or supper dish, especially amongst the men folk.

Culpeper's Herbal offers a mixed view on the virtues of boiled onions. '[They] are flatulent or windy, yet they somewhat promote appetite, increase thirst, ease the bowels, provoke women's courses, cureth the biting of the mad dog ...'

Carrot Pie

In winter the peaty potato fields between Liverpool and Rufford, and on Pilling and Cockerham Mosses, are visited by up to 30,000 pink-footed geese from Iceland. The geese do the potato farmers a great service by delving into the harvested fields and devouring tiny and broken bits of potato that would grow as weeds the following spring. In the early 1970s the area used for growing potatoes was greatly reduced and given over to growing carrots. The geese arrived back from Iceland, found sweet carrots growing in their favourite fields and they caused thousands of pounds of damage. One farmer claimed to have lost £7000-worth in one field in 1972. Today farmers keep an eye open and scare away any skeins of geese that attempt to form gaggles on the winter carrot fields.

Boiled carrots, sometimes boiled together with swede, mashed with lots of butter, is a traditional accompaniment with the Sunday joint. But the following recipe, by the late Mary Alice Stopforth of Burscough, is quite different. Burscough is in the centre of the south-west Lancashire carrot fields.

streaky bacon to every half pound of carrots. Put on top a short-crust pastry lid. Cook in a moderate oven for about 45 minutes. This pie is served with beef gravy.

On Sunday the family enjoyed roast beef and on Monday ate the rest of the beef cold. Carrot pie was put on the table on Tuesday, and the gravy may have included any leftovers from the two beef dinners.

Spring Greens

For pre-Industrial Revolution, rural Lancastrians the hardest time of the year as far as food availability was concerned was early spring. Then the supplies of salt pork, oatmeal, wheat flour, dried peas and beans, and potatoes would have been dwindling and their hens would be still 'off lay'. Spring was the time for sowing, not reaping. It is no coincidence that the Early Church chose this time of the year for Lent, the time of fasting. Why have a long period of fast when food is relatively abundant? However, families could eke out the last of their supplies by ingeniously exploiting the first flush of spring in the countryside around them.

'From Culpeper's Herbal: Dandelion or Piss-a-beds ... openeth the passages of the urine both in young and old ...'

The tips and leaves of young nettles, chickweed, orache, bistort, sorrel, water-cress, jack-by-the-hedge (also called garlic mustard because of its taste), goose grass and ransoms (or wild garlic, because it could be used instead of real garlic or onion), hawthorn and lime tree, could be boiled. The leaves of dandelions and fat-hen could be eaten raw as a salad. These wild plants are still good to eat.

Make a collection of wild spring greens. I would recommend a good variety, but with dandelion leaves and the youngest nettle shoots making up the bulk of them. Wash well and then simmer for ten minutes. Drain, season to taste, and then mash and chop the greens with a knob of butter. Finally, mix in one or two finely chopped hard-boiled eggs or serve with one poached egg per helping.

How to get the best fresh vegetables

The first way is to grow your own!

Most people do not realise how easy it is to produce a few vegetables at home. You don't even need to dig the garden. I grow every year, in containers, carrots, lettuces and a variety of salad leaves, dwarf French beans, courgettes, tomatoes, strawberries and melons. In one large container I have a fig tree that, last year, produced 47 of the most succulent figs imaginable! I also grow new potatoes (the old variety

Arran Pilot) in large plant pots and old buckets, planting the first sets in February that give us new potatoes early in May.

By having a vegetable bed you increase the variety that you can grow, and then it is wise to choose things that you especially like that which are usually expensive and which taste best when put straight into boiling water, such as broad beans, purple sprouting broccoli, and even asparagus.

The ultimate in home production is, of course, an allotment. When I had an allotment we were self-sufficient in most vegetables except for main crop potatoes. Allotments are very time consuming, but very satisfying. Why not share one with friends, then two or three families can enjoy vegetables at their best?

The best alternative to growing your own is to buy straight from the farmer at one of the new farm shops.

Diglake farm lies at the edge of the mosslands between Ormskirk and Scarisbrick. It takes its name from an ancient lake that was drained several hundred years ago and on which the farm was established. The Vose family moved here from another farm at Halsall in the 1920s, and Paul Vose now runs it. The farm is not a particularly large one, and its profitability is down to hard work on the land and selling what Paul produces through the farm shop.

Potatoes growing on the south-west Lancashire mosslands. Before they were reclaimed they would have looked like the moss on page 44.

'THE PRACTICE OF HAVING OUT-OF-SEASON VEGETABLES GROWN FOR A PITTANCE EXPLOITS THE THIRD WORLD COUNTRIES'

This is an aspect of modern farming that I encountered throughout Lancashire whilst gathering information for this book. Profit margins in agriculture have been greatly reduced in the last two or three decades, so that to make a reasonable income farmers have had to increase the size of their farms (an example is given on page 85), to add value to their basic product (for instance, milk and cheese, see page 86, or milk as ice cream, page 88) or sell directly to the public through a farm shop and miss out the middle-men. The Vose family converted a roadside barn into a shop and they sell what they grow.

Their crops are typical of those grown on all the Lancashire moss-lands.Potatoes take up a large acreage. The variety Ulster Prince is the first early grown by Paul and, to get as early (and profitable) a crop as possible he plants his first sets in a polytunnel, harvesting them in late May or very early June. In flavour these are at least the equal of the over-hyped Jersey Royal. Paul then plants the rest of his Ulster Prince sets in open fields in mid March and prays that they will not be burnt by late frosts. A second early variety, Maris Bard, follows the Ulster Prince and this is the main potato in the shop through the summer. Paul grows two main crop varieties that he sells by the pound and in 25kg bags from autumn through to the following spring. One of these I had never tasted until I bought a bag from Diglake three years ago. It is called Nadine and it makes the best baked potatoes and excellent roast potatoes. The other main crop potato that Paul grows is Maris Piper, an outstanding potato for making chips and a very good roaster.

6 From *Culpeper's Herbal:* "Boiled lettuce ... abateth bodily lust, outwardly applied to the testicles with a little camphire [camphor]." 9

Diglake Farm produces all the spring, summer and autumn cabbages sold in the shop the year round, and sprouts through autumn and winter. Paul also grows cauliflowers and broccoli, but not enough to satisfy year-round demand. So when his crop is finished he goes off to the wholesale market. Here he meets with a problem. Huge farms that supply supermarkets produce some of what he buys via

Paul Vose checking his first early potatoes.

the wholesale market. Supermarkets will only accept vegetables that match their often-idiotic standards of appearance (Paul told me of a supermarket buyer checking a sample of carrots with a micrometer!), so the big growers send their perfect cauliflowers to the supermarkets and try to off load less perfect cauliflowers via the wholesale market. So when Paul supplements his produce at the market, he must check carefully to ensure that what he buys is of the high quality of his own produce.

Paul grows sufficient onions to keep the shop supplied from late summer to late spring, leeks and beetroot the year round, peas, broad beans and French dwarf beans through summer, pumpkins at Halloween, marrows and courgettes in summer.

Which leads to taste and seasonality. We all happily accept that, in late spring and summer, there are no fresh sprouts on the market. If you want to eat sprouts with your roast chicken in June then it will have to be frozen sprouts.

In recent years, led by supermarkets, people have happily forgotten seasonality among fruit and vegetables. Dwarf beans, which are a summer crop here in Lancashire, are grown in Kenya the year round for the UK market. By the time they have reached the supermarket shelves they have lost most of their flavour and nutrients. Even worse, the practice of having out-of-season vegetables grown for a pittance in this way exploits Third World countries and countryside.

Asparagus is a speciality of Lancashire. Once, vast fields of asparagus grew around Formby and, if you look hard, you can still find farmers who grow asparagus and sell it in their farm shops. Lancashire

Lancashire asparagus: wonderful!

asparagus is cut and in season from early May to the 20th of June. Enjoy it then. The bits of green twig imported by supermarkets from Peru and elsewhere every month of the year taste nothing like real Lancashire asparagus, cooked on the day that it was cut.

Strawberries are summer fruits in Lancashire, and there are market gardeners in the county who, by using greenhouses and a little heat, have extended the season from May to October. Their strawberries are lusciously sweet. The tasteless, red ball bearings that masquerade as strawberries and are imported from far away are not real strawberries.

Why then do people buy them?

There is nothing like eating the best fruit and vegetables when they are in season, cooked as soon as possible after they have been harvested. Unless you grow your own, the best is bought from the farm that grew it, or from the market stall that buys fresh from the farm.

Samphire: a taste of the sea

Samphire is a low-growing fleshy plant that grows at the edges of saltmarshes on sandy mud. It occurs commonly between Southport pier and Marshside on the Ribble estuary and at the edges of several Morecambe Bay saltings. An annual, it is ready for gathering in late summer. If you don't want to go out there and gather your own, you can buy it fresh and pickled.

I like it fresh. As soon as you get home, wash the samphire in running water and then put into a large pan of boiling salted water. It will be cooked in a matter of minutes. Put the hot samphire in a warmed dish and dot butter on top. Season with a little salt and black pepper. To eat (with brown bread and a glass of chilled white wine) you take a sprig by the base, pop it in your mouth and, as you pull the woody core of the samphire out of your mouth, you suck off the juicy bits. Delicious!

Samphire, sometimes called sea asparagus, can be gathered at several places around the Lancashire coast in September. Boiled or pickled, it is delicious.

Black Peas (Parched Peas)

You will often find stalls selling black peas at fairs, circuses and open-air fairs, for black peas are an old favourite. Market stalls often sell the dried peas and they are ideal for a big family outdoor gathering. Try them before a summer barbeque.

Take a pound of black peas and soak them in a large pan of clean water for at least twelve hours. Drain and pour in lots of water, salt and a good helping of vinegar. Bring to the boil and then simmer for at least four hours (or until the peas are very tender). One serving is only a couple of ounces, hot, with vinegar. It's an old flavour of Lancashire!

Ready-to-eat, quality Lancastrian food at Bury market.

FRUIT

Roeships have always been an important source of Vitamin C.

FRUIT HAS BEEN AN INTEGRAL PART of our diet since Mesolithic hunter-gathers colonised Lancashire 7000 years ago. From at least Anglo-Saxon times have been produced cultivated varieties of apples, pears, plums (including damsons), gooseberries, blackcurrants and strawberries. Before fruit trees and bushes were brought into cultivation, many wild fruits were picked ... and they continue to be picked today.

Look hard and you will find wild raspberries and strawberries in secluded hedgerows and woodland that taste as sweet just as the cultivated, and perhaps more so.

Soft Fruits

Blackberries have been brought into cultivation and used to form hybrid fruits with other species (there are even thornless varieties that are easy to pick!). So today we have loganberries and tayberries, and the less well-known tummelberries, veitchberries and youngberries (crosses between blackberries, dewberries and raspberries). Visit a pick-your-own fruit farm and you will find these. They are ideal for jam making and for pies. However there are many wild blackberry patches in the county where the fruits can be gathered for nothing other than a little time and, perhaps, a few scratches. I grow three cultivated varieties of blackberry and have a short wild blackberry hedge, and to be honest I find the wild fruits far superior to the cultivated.

While some people still do gather wild blackberries, very few consider the wild rosehip harvest. In bygone days the ripe orange or red hips were gathered in autumn. They were halved and the hairy seeds removed. The orange flesh was then eaten, giving a boost to the vitamin C level in the body.

Two more important wild fruits were provided by the peaty moorlands and unreclaimed mosslands: the cranberry and the bilberry (called whimberry in Lancashire). Cranberries, of course have been brought into cultivation and used to make the cranberry sauce that goes with the Christmas turkey. Bilberry has not. Instead we find cartons of the American blueberry on supermarket shelves and blueberry plants for sale at garden centres. But these have a pathetic flavour when put alongside the wild bilberry. A few Lancastrians know this, and you will see them in summer with a basin in one hand and the other hovering over the low bilberry shrubs on the Rivington moors, on Longridge Fell and on the moorland slopes of Bowland. If you want to taste the finest of all fruit pies, collect some whimberries!

In the old days soft fruits would not keep for more than a day or two after picking, so they were eaten immediately. It was not until refined sugar became available in the nineteenth century that soft fruits could be stored as jam. The flavour could then be enjoyed for many months, though the boiling method in jam-making destroyed all the vitamin C. Today we can freeze fresh soft fruits, so a day spent in the pick-your-own fruit farm can be used to store a wide variety of fruits that will last through the winter. But, for those who have never before picked-their-own, be warned. Strawberries do not freeze well: they become mushy and have a slight metallic taste when thawed out. The best fruits for freezing are damsons, raspberries, blackberries (and their crosses), gooseberries, blackcurrants, red currants and white currants.

From *Culpeper's Herbal*. 'Bilberry … grows in the northern parts of this land, as Lancashire … [bilberries] do somewhat bind the belly, and stay the vomitings and loathings: the juices of the berries made into a syrup, or the pulp made into a conserve with sugar, is good for the purposes aforesaid, as also for an old cough, or an ulcer in the lungs, or other diseases therein.'

SUNDAY TEA AT THE VICARAGE

Sunday tea was different from any other meal of the week. Monday to Friday our main meal was eaten in the evening, when everyone got home from work or school. Saturday was a day with no pattern, when we went shopping, or watched Preston North End, or went for a walk into the country. Sunday *had* a distinct pattern. We went to church on Sunday morning and this was followed by a roast beef or lamb, two veg. and roast potato dinner. Then later, before going to the evening service, there was Sunday tea.

Sunday tea might start with sandwiches, or perhaps a salad with bread and butter on the side. The salad always included hard-boiled eggs, sliced with an egg slice, and with the salad there would be either boiled ham or tinned salmon. There then followed a selection of cakes that mother had baked the previous day and, in summer, strawberries or raspberries picked an hour earlier from the garden.

The problem with being the son of a vicar is that visiting preachers and their wives would join us for Sunday tea and might devour more than their fair share of cakes and fresh fruit. My two brothers and I solved this when raspberries were on the menu. Philip, my youngest brother and who, my grandmother insisted, had a cemented reservoir for a stomach, would finish his first course with time in hand. I would then serve him with his raspberries (these were organic raspberries, for we never sprayed them with insecticide). Then Philip would quickly dissect a few fruits,

remove the maggot-like larvae of the raspberry beetle from their centres, and lay them on the side of his bowl, reciting, 'Tinker, Taylor, Soldier ... !'

Our guests would then insist that they were too full for raspberries so we ate their share as well. Charles Caxton, who was then Bishop of Blackburn, always insisted that, 'I just cannot preach off a full stomach!'

Apples and Pears

Although we can buy pears in the shops and on the markets, they do not grow well in Lancashire. Pears need sunnier conditions than apples, they hate cold winds and because they flower earlier than apples there is a greater risk of frost preventing pollination. And when a pear tree produces a crop in Lancashire, the fruit will often be hard, and not with the sloppy lusciousness that we associate with the best pears.

Some very popular varieties of dessert apple also do not produce good crops in Lancashire. Cox's Orange Pippin and Golden Delicious are good examples of what varieties NOT to grow in your Lancashire garden, though many garden centres in the county sell them. There are many others that do crop well here.

As new varieties of apples were discovered, it was found that some were sweeter than others and that gave rise to a separation of apple varieties into tart cookers and sweet eaters. It was also found that some varieties do not keep at all, so they must be eaten straight from the tree, whereas others not only keep well in store but also actually improve with the keeping. So bear that in mind if you fancy growing one or two apple trees. This is possible in the smallest of gardens by purchasing trees on the dwarf rootstock M27 (these grow to only five or six feet tall). Recommended varieties are:

Discovery: a dessert apple that eats straight from the tree in August/ September. Does not keep.

Lord Lambourne: a dessert apple that, though picked in September, improves with keeping so that it eats best in October/November.

Egremont Russet: a delicious, nutty dessert apple that, though picked late in September, improves with keeping and eats well up to New Year. This also makes a good apple pie.

Lord Derby: a cooking apple that can be used immediately after being picked in late September.

Bramley's Seedling: the most popular cooking apple, which 'falls' with cooking so is the best for making apple sauce. Picked in October, the Bramley improves with keeping and is at its best from November onwards.

Lord Lambourne apples. The three varieties shown on these pages are ideal for growing in a Lancashire garden.

Lane's Prince Albert: an excellent cooking apple. Picked in October, the fruits will improve in store and last until March.

In his diaries, Nicholas Blundell gave details of his orchards near Crosby in the early years of the eighteenth century. As today, the grafting of edible varieties of apples on to crab apple rootstocks took place in March, just as the sap started to rise. On the 7th March 1704 Blundell noted: 'Thomas Tickley grafted amany Apple trees,' and on 23rd March 1721 he recorded that 'Jackson Planted me some Cabbage Plants, and trimmed most of my Frute Trees as came last from London, he grafted seaven sorts of Apples the whip-graft way on my Hodg-podg Tree in the New Ground.'

If space is a limiting factor in your garden, you can buy 'family trees' where two or three varieties have been grafted onto the one rootstock. To have seven different varieties on the one tree is probably a record!

Though Blundell's apple crop was harvested by mid autumn (on 6th October 1707 he noted, 'The last of my Apples were gathered'), they lasted well in store. On 3rd March 1705 he recorded, 'I sent two Paniers of Apples to Richard Cartwright to Leverpoole to be sold,' and on 11th March 1703, 'I sent Richard Ainsworth to Leverpoole with 10 Busshells of Apples to Bessy Peele.' Ten bushels is eighty gallons in volume, and a lot of apples.

Today gardeners and commercial fruit-growers protect their crops from insect pests. However, in the sixteenth and seventeenth centuries one of the greatest destroyers of fruit crops was the then very common bullfinch (called 'malpes' in Lancashire), which ate the opening fruit buds. Bullfinches were trapped, killed and then taken to the churchwarden who would pay a bounty for them. For instance, in the Prescot Churchwarden's Accounts for 1594 we read, 'Item, paid to Mathew Stemson for vij [seven] urchins [hedgehogs], xx [twenty] crowe heades, iij [three] mouldes [moles], iij malpes, ijs. id. [two shillings and a penny].' Bulfinches are now a fairly scarce bird in Lancashire.

Egremont Russet (below) and Lord Derby (below right).

The Pick-Your-Own Fruit Farm

Kenyon Hall Fruit Farm on Winwick Lane at Croft, a few miles north of Warrington, is the oldest and largest pick-your-own farm in the county and people 'in the know' make a pilgrimage often of many miles to collect all the fruit they need for the deep freeze or jam making. In May and June the farm is Lancashire's largest producer of asparagus. From mid June strawberries, gooseberries and rhubarb are ripe for picking and they are joined by raspberries, red currants, Tayberries, blackberries and blackcurrants in late June and early July. Picking finishes in August.

The farm shop at Kenyon Hall also provides other local produce including new potatoes, salad crops and garden peas and broad beans.

One advantage of picking-your-own is that the price you pay is far less than the price in the shops and supermarkets. But far more important is the quality and freshness. Strawberries picked and then eaten a couple of hours later taste far better than strawberries that have been picked, boxed, transported to a central distribution centre and then transported to the supermarket. And gooseberries that are put in the deep freeze within a couple of hours of picking produce far sweeter pies than gooseberries that have spent a couple of days getting to the shop.

Picking strawberries is fun; eating them is even better!

Crab Apple Jelly

There is a pool on the River Ribble called the Crab Apple Tree Pool. Every October the ripe crab apples fall from the tree that lends its name to the pool and, as a break from trying to catch a salmon, I use my landing net to catch the apples as they float downstream. A net full of crab apples produces enough crab apple jelly to last the winter. But you need not try to find the Crab Apple Tree Pool to collect the crab apples you need! There are lots of crab apples in the county … I know another by the Hodder … and, come to think of it, many neighbours have crab apple trees in their gardens. So, you could find your nearest crab apple tree and go scrumping!

Wash and chop the crab apples and for every three pounds that goes into the large jam pan pour in 1½ pints of water. Bring to the boil and simmer until the crab apples have turned to a soft pulp. That will take up to an hour.

Now filter off the juice through a nylon sieve. Do not force the juice through the sieve or the resulting jelly may be cloudy.

Back into the jam pan put the juice and, for every pint of juice, one pound of jam sugar. Dissolve the sugar and bring the juice to the boil. Boil rapidly for about ten minutes and then test to see if the setting point has been reached. Continue to boil and test until the setting point is reached.

Pour into warmed jars, label and allow to cool and set. The resulting jelly usually has a nice pink tinge. If you want more colour, add a handful of rowan (mountain ash) berries to the fruit when you are boiling it.

This jelly is excellent with lamb, game and smoked duck breast, the similarly made Bramble Jelly a great addition to pâtés and meat pies.

PIG AND PORK

'3 Feb. 1703 Mr Smith, Mr Richard Lathom & I went to Carr-Hall; we eat Eggs & Collops Etc.'

From The Great Diurnal of Nicholas Blundell.

A happy pig!

Note: Collops was the old name for bacon and, as the day before Ash Wednesday (the first day of Lent and the start of the forty days of fasting before Easter) was Shrove Tuesday, on which we still traditionally enjoy eating pancakes, so the day before Shrove Tuesday was Collops Monday, when the last red meat – bacon – was eaten before the fast.

THE PIG WAS THE COTTAGERS' chief source of meat when Lancashire was a rural county. It was easy to keep, for being omnivorous it would devour any waste from the kitchen, such as potato peelings and swede tops. It would also grub away in scrub or woodland close to the cottage for roots and leaves and, in autumn, acorns and beech mast. Of course, from medieval times landowners in whose woodland and scrubland the pigs grubbed for food sought some payment, and cottagers and hamlets used to pay for a 'right of pannage' – the right to have their pigs feeding on woodland fruits and seeds.

It is only in the last fifty years that the practice of keeping a pig for the family has been forced to die out. I have been told at both Hesketh Bank and West Leigh that during the Second World War pigs were kept illicitly in out-of-the-way corners of the farm or in a back yard. In autumn all those involved had a share of the pork. Had the authorities been aware of it that pork would have gone 'to the War Effort'. I remember well walking on my way to Kirkham and Wesham Junior

School, passing some allotments where there was a huge saddleback sow. In spring she farrowed a litter of six piglets, five of which were sold on. The one remaining grew fatter until the autumn when its owner had it slaughtered. I missed that pig, for it delighted in eating the waxed paper bags that had held my breakfast corn flakes!

Those who owned a pig would collect the 'swill', or food waste (peelings, scrapings from plates etc.), from families around who didn't keep a pig. This swill was boiled up with a few oats, wheat or potatoes before being fed to the pig. The aim was always to produce the fattest pig possible, for the fat was vitally important as it could be rendered down to produce lard that was, until we became health-food conscious, the main fat for all cooking purposes. For instance, pastry made with lard tastes far better than pastry made with other forms of fat. Today's lean pigs ideally weigh in at 130–140 lbs (60kg); a hundred years ago you aimed to get the pig to 200 lbs (90kg) or more if you could.

But then the Nanny State and European Union intervened with regulations that made the keeping and then slaughtering of a family pig well nigh an impossibility, and another traditional aspect of life was lost.

In autumn the fattened pig would be led to its demise close to the cottage door. This is where the expression 'being led up the garden path' comes from. There it was tethered tightly. It has been said that a bucket was held over the pig's head so that it couldn't see what the future held. It was then stunned, its throat cut, and the blood collected to make black puddings (page 73). The carcass was then laid on and covered with straw, which was set alight to burn off the pig's bristles. This, it is said, produces far tastier crackling than we get with the current method of shaving off the bristles.

‘In autumn the fattened pig would be "led up the garden path" to its demise at the cottage door’

The pig was then suspended by its hind legs, perhaps from the bough of an apple tree. Its guts were removed carefully. The liver and heart might be cooked later that day. The intestine lining was used to make the skins for sausages and black puddings, the muscle to make chitterlings and the fat around the gut (called *poolings*) peeled away to go to the lard. The membranes holding the intestine in place and known as *veil* were used to enclose faggots. The body cavity would be lined by thick layers of fat that could be peeled away in flat slabs called *leaf.* That was the chief source of fat to be rendered down into lard. Then the head was removed and, usually, used to make brawn, though sometimes it might be roasted and made the centrepiece in some great celebration.

The carcass was then split lengthways into two halves. Sometimes the halves would be treated differently. One half might be butchered into joints of fresh meat – foreleg, hind leg, rib of pork, belly of pork and pork chops – for roasting and grilling. These could not be kept for long in the days before deep-freezers, so they would have to be sold or shared with others. However, by staggering the time of slaughter of their pigs, several families might have a joint of fresh pork each week through the late autumn and early winter.

The majority of the pork, however, was cured so that it would last the family through the winter and the following spring. The pig was jointed, the front leg becoming the fore ham, the hind leg the gammon ham, while the sides became bacon and the belly salt pork. So important was this salted and cured meat that the Lancashire nickname for the pig was the *bacon-tree*.

> 'THE LANCASHIRE NICK-NAME FOR THE PIG WAS THE *BACON-TREE*'

Curing was done with salt. After preparation, each joint was covered with a mix of 50 parts of salt to one part of saltpetre (this kept the joints a nice pink colour). A fortnight later the joints were wiped and re-salted. The larger joints might then be left in the salt for as long as a month. During salting the meat would lose about ten percent of its weight in the form of water. The joints were then wiped dry and hung in a warm room, and as they continued to dry a further five percent of weight would be lost in the form of water. Some cottages had chambers built in the side of the chimney where the salted joints could be hung and take extra flavour from the peat or wood fire burning down below.

But even cured pork was not immune to pests. In a letter dated March 30 1771 Gilbert White wrote that, 'There is a small long shining fly in these parts very troublesome to the housewife, by getting into the chimnies, and laying its eggs in the bacon while it is drying: these eggs produce maggots called jumpers, which, harbouring in the gammons and best parts of the hogs, eat down to the bone, and make great waste.'

To a poor cottager such a loss would be catastrophic.

Most large pieces of fat were rendered down to make lard, the clear fat being poured into the pig's stomach or small jars and stored in a cool place. Some fat was added to the blood in the black puddings. Any scraps of meat produced during butchery were minced to make sausages. The pig's feet or trotters were boiled and then fried. Nothing was wasted from the pig other than, it is said, its squeal. An old Lancashire joke denied this: Leyland Motors used the squeal in their brakes!

Today most of the pork that we eat is roasted (joints) or grilled (chops, gammon) or fried (bacon, sausages) or boiled (black puddings, hams). That was not the case a hundred and more years ago. Then most pork was cured and small amounts added to dishes of potatoes or other fairly bland foods to add a little flavour. If you would like to try one of these old dishes, try this:

Take a rasher of smoked streaky bacon and chop it up finely. Fry a level teaspoon of this in lard until it is brown. Now pour in some pancake batter (from 4 oz flour, ½ pint milk, 2 eggs, 2 pinches salt) and make a pancake in the usual way. When you come to eat the pancake it will taste of bacon, despite such a small amount of bacon in there. One rasher will be enough to flavour eight pancakes.

> '*NOTHING WAS WASTED FROM THE PIG OTHER THAN ITS SQUEAL*'

Even simpler was *dip*, the Lancashire name for salt pork or bacon fat, melted in a pan, into which bread or oatcakes would be dipped.

See also Bacon Shapes, and Pondoaf or Stirabout, page 39.

A slice of bacon in rural Lancashire used to be called a *sward* or a *shive*. Two Woodplumpton farmers that I knew in the early 1960s frequently invited me in for 'baggin', which at mid-morning was 'a bacon sward and a cup of tea'.

Pigs' Ears

Put the ears in a pan of boiling water and simmer for about 40 minutes. While the ears are cooking prepare some stuffing (if you wish you may use a packet stuffing such as chestnut and cranberry, or if you prefer it make your own). Let the ears cool and then slip a blunt knife under the skin on the inside (concave side) of each ear and fill the cavity with stuffing. Fry until brown on both sides.

Brawn

Take a pig's head, split in half with the brain removed, and four pigs' feet and soak in salty water for 24 hours. Some recipes also included the pig's heart. Then put head and feet (and heart if used) into a large pan with one large peeled onion, three carrots and two sliced turnips. Season with salt and pepper and put in a bouquet garni (or a helping of dried mixed herbs). Cover with water, bring to the boil and simmer for three hours, skimming off any froth from the surface.

Remove all meat from the bones. If the meat stubbornly remains attached to the bones, simmer for another half hour or so until it comes away.

> Pour the stock through a fine sieve into a clean pan, add the juice of a lemon or two tablespoons of vinegar, and bring to the boil. Simmer until the volume is reduced by half. Chop all the meat finely and add to the stock. Pour into a mould (a loaf tin will do) and leave to cool and set.

Go to one of the great Lancashire markets and you will find brawn for sale. Try it. It is delicious with a salad or in a sandwich.

Pigs' Feet (or Trotters)

> Wash them thoroughly and then put them in a pan of boiling water. Simmer until the meat comes easily from the many small bones (about 2 hours). Take the pieces of meat, dip into either seasoned flour or batter, and fry until brown. Superb!

Harry Shorrock tells me that during the Second World War, when cinemas were the chief source of entertainment other than the radio, a Preston women spent every afternoon and evening in the cinema chewing and sucking boiled then fried pigs' feet with the bones still in them!

Pea and Pigs' Feet Soup

> Soak 8 oz of dried peas in a large bowl of water overnight.
>
> Drop six trotters into a large pan containing three pints of boiling water and simmer for up to two hours until the meat separates easily from the many bones. Put the meat to one side, discarding the bones, and sieve the stock into a clean pan.
>
> Add the soaked peas and two large chopped carrots to the stock, bring to the boil and simmer until peas and carrots are well cooked. Add the meat, season with salt and pepper, and enjoy it.

The more widely known pea-and-ham soup is made in precisely the same way using a ham shank from the butchers.

If you make your own boiled ham the stock produced can be used to make a good pea soup. Simply add 8 oz of dried peas that have been soaked overnight and two chopped carrots to every two points

of stock. When the soup is cooked, put in a few small pieces of the boiled ham.

This fairly thick soup – it really is a rib-sticker – freezes very well and makes a great lunch after a winter's morning walking in Bowland or around one of the many great Lancashire nature reserves.

Black Pudding

The best black puddings are said to come from Bury and, if you visit Bury's magnificent market, you will find that many Lancastrians agree. There you will see two stalls, one belonging to The Bury Black Pudding Company, the other to Chadwicks, where customers form long queues as they wait to buy some.

The essential ingredient of black pudding is pigs' blood, but there is far more in the concoction.

First pearl barley and groats (hulled, cushed oats) are boiled until they are very soft. They are then taken from the hot water and mixed with seasoning, flour, finely chopped onion and small pieces of pork fat. This mix is then stirred into the pig's blood and the whole slightly thickened with fine oatmeal.

The final mix is injected into pieces of intestine lining. Originally this was from the pig, though today the intestines from bullocks are also used. The puddings are then shaped, tied with string, and lowered into simmering water for 20 minutes.

Many twenty-first century Lancastrians worry about cholesterol and saturated animal fats, so the major manufacturers produce very low fat black puddings as well as the traditional ones. That saves the eater from having to dissect out the bits of fat. There is also a small black pudding called the 'breakfast berry' to eat with your eggs and bacon.

In theory black puddings are already cooked and some people do eat them cold, as they were bought. Most of us who enjoy black puddings prefer them hot, boiled in a pan of water for ten minutes or halved lengthways and either grilled or fried. As a supper dish, eaten with mustard or, better still, Lancashire sauce, they are delicious.

Lancashire Sauce

This is an old recipe of the Entwistle family of Bridge Street, Ramsbottom. Its contents are entirely natural: water, vinegar, caramel, coriander, turmeric, fenugreek, cumin, fennel, gram dhal, English mustard, garlic, sugar, black pepper and salt. You can buy bottles of it from Entwistle's delicatessen or from the black pudding stalls on Bury market. It is lovely with all forms of cooked ham and sausages as well as the black pudding.

Lancashire sausages of the twenty-first century

We Lancastrians get other county's sausages thrust down our throats! Every butcher and supermarket, it seems, sells Cumberland or Wiltshire sausages, suggesting that Lancastrian sausages do not exist. But they do.

If you want to see sausage perfection it is essential to go to Clitheroe, the town that is nearest to the geographical centre of Britain. For there the Cowman family run 'The Original Farm Sausage Shop'.

Cliff Cowman and his famous sausage shop.

Cliff, who now manages the shop, is the fifth in the family to have done so. Every Cowman's sausage is made at the back of the shop on Castle Street, using the finest quality pork from free-range pigs sourced in Lancashire. Altogether Cliff sees between 600 and 800 kg (1300–1750 lbs) of pork processed and sold as sausages every week.

When I called at the shop there were 39 different varieties of sausage on display behind the glass counter, a further 19 in the window display, and hidden away in cold store were nine special and seven gluten-free varieties. Lancashire Pork sausage is the special family-secret mix, but if you want a jumbo sausage then you will choose Giant Pork. If you would like to combine Lancashire pork with another of our famous tastes, then there is Pork and Black Pudding. Clitheroe Hot 'N' Spicy came about when a customer wanted something with a bit of a kick in it. It's too hot for me. I would prefer, for a change, Pork and Walnut or Pork and Apricot, especially with roast chicken. Something special for Christmas? You must try Ted's Christmas Special (invented by Cliff's father), or Pork and Plum (goes with goose), or Pork, Cranberry and Rosemary (with turkey).

Cliff will even produce a batch of sausages for a special occasion. Some years ago he made up some Pork and Baked Bean sausages for a school fund-raising effort and later some Pork and Banana sausages for a barbeque at another school.

These are sausages with both the old flavour of Lancashire and the new!

The old pork of Lancashire, today!

Most of the pigs that are butchered and sold as pork are raised in dreadful conditions, bred and fed for the production of cheap, lean and relatively tasteless meat. They are far removed from the pigs that scratched out a living in the forest or were fed on the delicious mix that was pigs'-swill.

In 1993 Phillip and Louise Edge set up a 2000-strong pig farm in the Ribble valley at Osbaldeston (intensive pig farms usually have 30–50,000). Unfortunately the business was not generating enough income as the quality of pork they were producing was not rewarded by the middlemen through whom they were selling their pigs. And of course the middlemen were taking a big slice of the profit from their pigs. So they decided to cut out the middlemen by butchering the pork themselves and selling directly to the public.

Their pig-herd is a cross between a Large White and a Landrace. This produces a consistently high quality, fine-tasting pork. Both boars and sows of each breed used to produce the pigs that they butcher and sell are raised on the farm so that there is no possibility of any disease affecting them through contact with pigs from other

Philip and Louise Edge.

farms. This means that they have a 'closed herd' and that they need use no drugs.

Phillip was solely a farmer and, though he knew a lot about raising pigs, he knew nothing of preparing them for the consumer. They were fortunate. One of their neighbours, Ken Turner, had been an expert butcher and he taught Phillip how to butcher the carcass, make sausages, and cure bacon and ham. So all the pork products that are sold at their Fairfield Farm shop by the A49 is grown, butchered and prepared on the farm. The outcome is that the purchaser obtains top-quality pork, from pigs that have had a contented life, without a premium added to the price that goes with the often misused term 'Organic'.

Many other farms in the Ribble valley have also benefited, for Phillip and Louise now butcher and sell beef and lamb from nearby farms (and they will happily tell you which farm the beef or lamb you are buying was raised) where animal welfare is a top priority and the product top class.

Louise added one other point: without the loyalty of many customers, their farm-shop could not continue to exist.

There are many other farm shops of this high standard in Lancashire. Any reader who enjoys good meat from farms where animal welfare is a priority should get their meat there.

> ## 'PERFECT' PORK
>
> Tender and Succulent
> 3 Pork Loin Steaks
> With added water, glucose, phosphates and salt to enhance succulence.
> *Label on a cut of pork in Sainsbury's supermarket, Leigh, 11 May 2006.*
>
> Yes, well, mmm!

MUTTON AND LAMB

ON 3RD APRIL 1277 the Cartulary of Burscough Priory listed the following as acceptable Lent offerings and tithes to the priory: hay, pigs, geese, garlic, leeks, wool and apples.

Beef is not mentioned, nor is mutton or lamb, though sheep's wool appears. The reason for this is that neither figured very much in the medieval Lancashire diet. In those days sheep were primarily a source of wool and following the Norman conquest of England the hills of northern England were converted into great sheep farms by the new Cistercian monasteries. Monks, who had abandoned an earlier foundation by the Mersey estuary, founded Whalley Abbey in the Ribble valley in 1296. Sawley Abbey was founded in 1147 as an offshoot of Fountain's Abbey. In 1124 Tulketh (now part of Preston) was founded by the Savigny Order, which moved to found Furness Abbey, between Barrow and Dalton, in 1124. And in about 1190 the Premonstratensian Order built Cockersand Abbey by the Lune estuary. In 1147 the Savigny and Premonstratensian orders became part of the Cistercian Order. These four religious houses controlled vast tracts of land in north Lancashire, Cumbria and the West Riding of Yorkshire for grazing their sheep, and so great was the profit that they were able to fund the construction of those magnificent buildings that we see today in ruins. The profit was, however, in wool, not meat.

By the beginning of the seventeenth century mutton appeared, roasted and boiled, on the table set before James I at Hoghton Tower (see page 3), and there is no doubt that cheese and butter made from ewes' milk was being made then in the county. Today, like the rest of the country, we enjoy roast leg or shoulder of lamb or grilled cutlets. But the published Lancashire recipes include the less expensive cuts, including the sheep's head and feet, and the cheapest neck chops in hot pot (page 45). It is clear that most Lancastrians up to the end of the nineteenth century – and for many well in to the twentieth century – never ate the finest parts of the sheep, and had to make do with the rest.

Sheep's Feet

> Take twelve sheep's feet, wash well, and simmer in four pints of water for about three hours, topping up the water from the boiled kettle when necessary. Remove the feet and take the meat off the bones; if the meat does not come away easily, boil for a bit longer. Sieve the stock into a clean pan.
>
> Peel and finely chop two onions, two carrots and a turnip and add to the stock with a few herbs (dried mixed herbs are fine). Season with salt and pepper. Bring to the boil and simmer for an hour, until the vegetables are well cooked and the volume of stock reduced.
>
> Thicken the resulting broth with a heaped tablespoon of plain flour mixed with a little butter. Then add the meat from the sheep's feet.

This is a very good broth and worth trying if you can find a butcher who sells sheep's feet. Try the old-style market stalls at places like Leigh and Bury.

Sheep's Head

> Take a clean sheep's head and soak it in water for at least four hours, changing the water at least twice.
>
> Put the head in a large pan, cover with water, add some chopped vegetables (e.g. three onions, carrots and turnips, a parsnip, two sticks of celery) and bring to the boil and simmer for three to four hours. Take the meat from the bones, including tongue and brain, cut into bite-sizes pieces and serve with mashed potatoes.

You can cook pig's and calf's heads in exactly the same way … if you can get hold of one! Health scares and Nanny State, together with the understandable squeamishness of the urban population, have seen these vanish during the late fifty years. Yet many older people can remember these as being a common and enjoyable dish.

Sheep's Head Soup

During the 1960s many biology students were encouraged to buy a sheep's head from their butcher and boil it for several hours until the meat fell off the bone and they had a clean skull to study. The stock from this operation was poured down the sink. What a waste!

Take a sheep's head and split it in half (the butcher will do this for you) and remove the brains. They go in a separate dish (see below).

Wash the head well and then put it in a large pan, cover with water, bring to the boil and simmer for about four hours. Keep the water level topped up from the kettle. Remove the head; the meat should drop off the bone. If not, continue to simmer until it does.

Pour the stock through a sieve into a clean pan and add ten washed and sliced leeks and two chopped carrots. Simmer for another hour. Thicken the soup by stirring in either stale bread or a paste of fine oatmeal and water. Put the meat back in and serve.

Sheep's Brains

You need about one pound of brains to feed four people. Soak in cold water for 4–6 hours, changing the water every hour. Before cooking peel away the surrounding membrane.

Cook in enough water to cover the brains, by slowly bringing the pan just to simmering point and poach for about 20 minutes (for sheep's or pig's brain; 25 minutes if you have managed to get a calf's brain and are cooking that). Under no circumstances must the water boil. Let the brains cool down in the water.

> Then, cut the brains into bite-sized pieces and either:
> Dip in whisked egg, then bread crumbs, and shallow fry.
> Or, dip in batter and deep fry.
> Serve with salad and a slice of lemon.

The thought of eating brains may sound revolting to the modern mind, but if you were presented with it cooked, without knowing what it was, you would almost certainly enjoy it!

Mutton Broth

This very early dish used any old scrawny sheep, though today we would use an inexpensive cut from the modern lamb.

> Take two pounds of finely chopped mutton or three pounds of neck of lamb chops. Put these in four pints of water and add a large sliced onion and turnip, two sliced carrots, a heaped tablespoon of pearl barley and seasoning. Bring to the boil and simmer for about three hours, topping up the water from the kettle when necessary and skimming off any froth that accumulates on the surface.

This broth was served in bowls with Lancashire oatcakes.

Producing prime Lancashire lamb

The hill sheep of Lancashire belong to one or other of a short list of tough breeds that can tolerate the often-foul weather on the tops and eke out a living from the tough pasture. One, the Lonk, is an old Lancashire breed, but increasingly Swaledale or Rough Fell have been used in lamb production. The male lambs produced in the upland flocks go to market, while the ewes are mated with a tup of a different breed that has been selected for growth rate and for flavour in the final meat. For his flock of ewes in the Hodder Valley, John Hartley chooses the Blue-faced Leicester.

The male offspring from this cross again go to market. The ewes, called 'mules', are taken from the higher pastures to lower land where they are tupped by a ram from one of the great meat-producing breeds. For this cross John prefers the Suffolk, though the French breed Charollais or the Dutch breeds Texel and Meltexal are being increasingly used. It is the offspring of this cross that now produces the best-flavoured and leanest lambs for the table. And this is what you should be buying from the top farm-shops in Lancashire.

One question that many people ask is, how can fresh lamb (as distinct from frozen lamb) be available twelve months of the year?

The ruins of Salley (Sawley) Abbey. It was the income from sheeps' wool, not meat, that funded the building of the once-fine Cistercian buildings.

Two factors come into play: when the lamb is born and the food it eats.

The gestation period of a sheep is five months. In the milder parts of England, including the West Lancashire lowlands, the tup can be put to the ewes in August so that their lambs are born at New Year, but that does include extra costs as lambing in mid winter usually takes place indoors. Conditions are not suitable on higher ground for early lambing, so there the tup is put with the ewes as late as November so that the lambs are born in April (John added that, traditionally, lambing in hill sheep in Bowland begins on the 10th of April).

So some of the earliest new season lambs begin to appear in the butchers' shops in May or early June: this is the expensive 'spring lamb'. Many lambs born in the hills may be taken to lowland farms to be fattened – Bowland lambs may go to pastures on the Fylde or close to Morecambe Bay – and they appear on the market in late summer and autumn. This, John pointed out, is when lamb is at it cheapest and is the best time to get one for the freezer. And the last lambs to be born in any one year may continue to be fattened up through the winter to provide a source that will last until the next spring lambs appear.

As to flavour, the finest lamb that I have ever eaten was on Fair Isle in the Shetland Isles. That lamb had grown up on fairy tough grass and herbs as well as lots of nutritional seaweed that it had grazed from the strand line on the beach. It had been born in April 1986 and we ate it at Fair Isle Bird Observatory in August 1987, so it was quite old for a lamb and perhaps technically mutton. The finest Lancashire lamb that I have ever eaten (a mule x Suffolk cross) had been fattened on a Morecambe Bay saltmarsh. There it had grazed on saltmarsh grass and red fescue grass and it was delicious. If you can source a lamb fattened on saltmarsh grasses, that is the best.

Alas, mutton is very difficult to find in Lancashire. There are three reasons for this. The first is that the demand for lamb is so great that there is none left to be fed on for another year. The second is that because lambs must be kept a long time if they are to be marketed as mutton, mutton would be more expensive than lamb. The third is that most people imagine mutton to be tough and stringy, so that there is no demand.

In fact, a good quality lamb (for example, a mule x Suffolk cross) that has been grazing grass all its life tastes better and has a finer texture when mutton at 18 months than a lamb at three or four months.

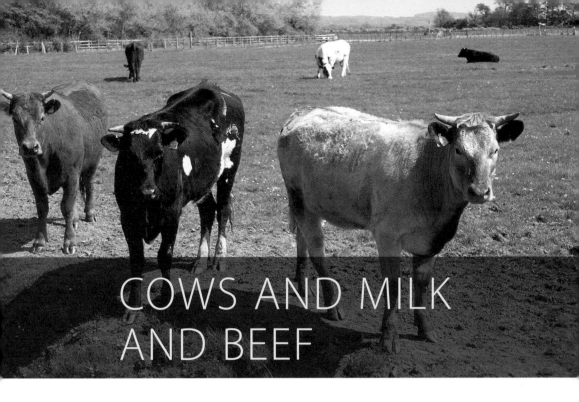

COWS AND MILK AND BEEF

WHEN I WAS A BOY AT KIRKHAM in the 1950s I used to go to watch Bickerstaffe's dairy herd being milked. Slowly the cows processed into the shippon (never 'byre' in Lancashire), as great a mix of forms and colour as could be imagined. Most were brown-and-white shorthorns, though why they were called shorthorns goodness only knows. Their horns seemed long enough to me. There was one, more delicate looking, Ayrshire, several nondescript cross-breeds, and three bad-tempered Jerseys with long eyelashes. They were there to up the fat content of the milk. Then in 1956 Mr Bickerstaffe bought two new black-and-white cows. These were the first Friesians I had ever seen. I haven't seen a shorthorn for years other than at shows. I know of a couple of specialists in the county who keep Ayrshires and Jerseys. And even the Friesian has gone, to be replaced by a similar black-and-white breed, but with a far deeper rear-end and bigger milk yield: the Holstein.

This swing away from farms having several breeds in their herds, that gave variable quantities of milk but often with milk having a high protein and butterfat content, to herds with a single, uniform breed, was driven by two factors. The first was that farmers were suddenly encouraged to have intensively bred cattle selected for high yield using artificial insemination with semen from top class bulls. The second was that, before the Second World War and the establishment of the Milk Marketing Board, many Lancashire farms produced milk that was primarily for turning into butter or cheese. The cheese and butter were easier to transport to the towns, had a longer shelf life and greater profit. Volume of milk, sold to the consumer in the pint bottle delivered to the door and, later, the plastic carton from the supermarket, suddenly became important in the 1940s.

In the old days the smaller towns and villages were supplied with milk straight from the farm. After morning milking the farmer or his wife would set out with a horse and cart carrying big metal milk churns (also called *kits* in Lancashire) and some metal half pint, pint and quart measures with long handles. The housewife would take out into the street a jug and the farmer would pour into the jug the required volume of milk.

In the larger towns and cities there were 'milk-houses'. Recently calved cows would be transported by wagon from the farm to a milk-house, fed on hay and cereals, milked twice every day and the milk sold to people in the streets around for their tea, puddings, custards etc. Then when the cow ran dry it would be taken back to the farm and a new in-milk cow sent to replace it.

But then, beginning in the 1930s but especially after the Second World War, cereals became the staples for breakfast requiring large quantities of milk. Instead of eating porridge made with water, children were increasingly fed things like Cornflakes and Rice Crispies and poured over their bowlful a quarter pint of milk. In addition, every schoolchild was given a gill of milk to drink at school every morning. The demand for readily available liquid milk mushroomed. Dairy farmers were paid by the volume and also for the fat and protein content of the milk their cows produced. Unproductive breeds vanished and the great milk producing Holstein became the dominant breed.

I asked John Hartley from Bashall Eaves to explain how the modern dairy farmer runs his herd.

A cow's gestation period is nine moths. So if you inseminate a cow on 15th June this year – go back three months … 15th May … 15th April … 15th March … and forward one week – its calf will be born on 22nd March next year.

Today farmers aim to have calves born

John Hartley. An expert dairy and sheep farmer.

throughout the year to guarantee a steady supply of milk. And instead of running any old bull with the herd, artificial insemination (AI) is used, using the semen from one of the genetically top bulls at the AI Centre. These bulls have been selected because their genes will increase the yield or quality of the milk their female calves will produce when they grow up and join the herd. Semen from these top bulls is collected about three times every week. Each collection of semen is divided into many units, each of which can fertilise a cow's egg, and the units are stored frozen in liquid nitrogen until required. The semen from a top bull may then be used to fertilize far more cows than the same bull could if left with one large herd. Some bulls have produced more than a million inseminations, and calves.

When a cow produces a calf her first milk is known as 'beastings'. At one time people sought beastings as it was reckoned to make the best custard. However Nanny State has made it illegal for beastings to be used for human use. After four days the cow is then taken into the herd and her milk goes into the tank and to market with the rest. She will then give milk for ten months before running dry. But three months after giving birth that cow can be inseminated to produce her next calf.

'IN THE OLD DAYS THE SMALLER TOWNS AND VILLAGES WERE SUPPLIED WITH MILK STRAIGHT FROM THE FARM'

The average Holstein produces about 25 litres of milk every day, though on farms with top quality grass (in summer) and silage (in winter), and by feeding the best cereal concentrates, the average yield can approach 30 litres per day. Milk as it comes from the cow will contain about 4% fat, much of it in the cream. However the companies that buy the milk from the farmers and bottle it remove some of the cream so that 'full cream milk' in the shops and supermarkets has 3.1% fat. One might imagine that semi-skimmed milk is milk with half the cream removed (and have 2% fat). This is not so. Milk with an already reduced 3.1% fat is mixed 50:50 with fully skimmed milk to give semi-skimmed milk. And we pay extra for the cream that has been skimmed off to make our trifles and cream cakes!

The price of milk and cream is now as low as it has ever been, so the profit per litre to the farmer small. Despite the great improvement in machinery, the improved winter feeding with silage instead of hay, the improved quality of grass in meadow and pasture, and the genetic improvements in the cows, 'All dairy farmers in the Ribble and Lune valleys are working harder – starting sooner in the morning and finishing later at nights – than their fathers did,' John told me. 'To make a reasonable income for our two families my brother and I are farming as a single farm what was four farms when my father started here, fifty years ago.'

Mrs Kirkham's Lancashire Cheese

Graham Kirkham's mother started making cheese on their farm at Goosnargh in the mid 1970s when the profit from liquid milk was falling. When I called Graham had just returned from the Specialist Cheesemakers' Association annual meeting at Truro, where Prince Charles had presented him with the 2006 trophy for Best British Raw Milk Cheese (i.e. real cheese). His is now accepted worldwide as the best Lancashire cheese, though as Graham pointed out, there are many other producers of real Lancashire cheese almost as good. Worldwide? About 40% of production is retailed through London and much of the rest is flown to the USA. You must look hard to find Mrs Kirkham's Lancashire cheese in the county: the farmers' markets at weekend in Liverpool and Manchester, Booth's Supermarket (that is also Lancashire's Supermarket and sources much of its fresh produce in the county), and the Port of Lancaster Smokehouse at Glasson Dock.

'Seek great traditional food in Lancashire and you will find it'

Cheese starts with milk, and Mrs Kirkham's milk comes from the family's herd of 80 milking Holsteins. The evening milking is pumped into a large tank where it is cooled and kept overnight. The following morning's milk is pumped into the same tank and the temperature raised. To this milk are then added a special starter (a family secret ingredient) and some calves' rennet. 'You could use vegetable rennet, but it is not as good,' insisted Graham. The rennet coagulates the milk, quickly separating the curds from the whey. They whey is then drained away to feed the calves, leaving the dense, creamy

Curds and whey being separated.

white curds that resemble a thick layer of soft cheese. To speed up drainage, Graham cuts and turns the curds. It is hot work. He wipes the sweat from his brow. The curds could be used as they are to make a soft cheese like the French Brie or Camembert. But Lancashire is a hard cheese, and that takes extra work.

In two adjacent tanks Graham has two-thirds of the previous day's curds and a third of the curds from the day before that. He now takes a third of today's curds and adds a third of each of the previous two days' curds to it. So any of Mrs Kirkham's Lancashire

Graham Kirkham and his assistant Fiona and some of their cheeses.

cheeses is a mix of three days' curds, one of which would have developed and dried for two days, one for one day, with the third fresh and raw. This is the part of cheese making that makes a great Lancashire cheese the best hard cheese. In days gone by Leigh Toaster was considered the premier Lancashire cheese; its wonderful texture and flavour came from this combination of ages of curds. Alas, Leigh Toaster, that got its name because it was popularly cooked, has been extinct for decades.

The three lots of curd are put through a peg-mill to mix them and break them up. Salt is then added and the curds again milled and mixed. Then the infant cheese is put in moulds and cheese pressed to squeeze out more whey and make the cheese firm. Each cheese is then wrapped in a muslin cloth and pressed for a further 24 hours. At this stage many hard cheeses are covered with wax. Instead, Mrs Kirkham's cheese is wiped over with melted butter to encourage the production of a protective rind. Finally, the cheese goes into store.

Cheese stalls on the markets will often have 'Crumbly Lancashire', 'Strong' or 'Tasty Lancashire' or 'Mild Lancashire'. 'It's all the same cheese,' Graham explained. 'It's simply a matter of how long it is allowed to mature. We aim for two to three months.' And he took a sample from a cheese made three months earlier and invited me to taste it. It was cheese perfection. Slightly creamy, nicely acidic, not too dry.

'How much cheese do you make in a day?' I asked.

'Usually eighteen cheeses, each weighing ten kilos.'

'And the milk comes only from your cows?'

'That's our limit. We use only our own milk, unpasturised, straight from the cow. We cannot buy milk in from other farms.'

'And how much does your cheese vary in taste?'

'Our best cheese – the absolute top – comes from autumn milk. The cows have been out all summer with the sun on their backs and are inside, eating the first of the silage. They are as fit as they can be. Their diet is controlled and perfect. Their milk is at its best.'

'So why don't you sell all your cheese in Lancashire? Why London and America?'

'There are lots of people making good, and sometimes excellent, Lancashire cheese in Lancashire. We have the edge, and can get a better price in London and the US.'

Graham concluded our discussion with a statement that is so right as far as all real food is concerned:

'People are increasingly looking for top quality food, and if you make top quality traditional food they will travel miles to find you.'

Seek great traditional food in Lancashire and you will find it. As I hope this book demonstrates, it is out there now!

Savoury Cheese was a popular dish and very easy to make. It is the origin of the name of the extinct cheese Leigh Toaster.

Mix some grated or finely chopped good Lancashire cheese, some chopped streaky bacon and a little chopped onion. Put the mix on a metal plate and stick it under a hot grill until the cheese is melted and getting a toasted brown top. Smear thickly on toast or fresh bread. A working man might have this for his evening meal when he returned home, but then a hole would be made in the centre of the uncooked cheese, bacon and onion mix and an egg put in the hole. Then the dish would be put under the grill until the cheese was toasted and egg softly cooked.

Cheese-potatoes were also a popular dish in the days when meat was relatively expensive and eaten only in tiny amounts.

Boil, drain, and then mash some potatoes (use a little milk if the potatoes are dry). Grate in some Lancashire cheese and mix thoroughly. Put in a dish, sprinkle the top with more grated cheese and put under a hot grill until the top is nicely browned.

Mrs Dowson's Ice Cream

For decades the dominant ice cream sold in Lancashire was predominantly mass-produced and far removed from the cream produced by cows. Today there are a very few farmers in Lancashire who are making real

Amanda and Eric filling tubs by hand with kibbled Uncle Joe's Mintballs ice cream.

ice cream. Eric and Amanda Dowson are among them.

In 2001 foot-and-mouth disease hit the Ribble Valley and though their milking stock survived, other stock held on fields adjacent to farms that suffered from the disease were (needlessly) slaughtered. The result was that the Dowson's were finding it difficult to pay their bills and they were left with only two alternative solutions: to sell-up or to move into some other more profitable venture. They chose the latter and decided that, instead of all their milk being sold for a pittance, they would use it to make ice cream.

'We sampled ice cream from every source we could find, said Amanda. 'Eric and the children were eating ice cream until it was coming out of their ears!' And through this painful testing and talking with other producers and potential consumers they learnt what was demanded of the market: 'a smooth and creamy high butterfat ice cream without a fatty or oily aftertaste.'

They commenced production in 2002 with just seven flavours, one of them chocolate. The first three batches of chocolate were tested on their children's now well-trained palettes. The children said, 'No!' and the pigs enjoyed the three batches of ice cream.

Initially the Dowsons sold their ice cream through local shops and cafes, but by 2006 they were producing 53 flavours, including eight sorbets, with retail outlets across Lancashire. Several leading restaurants now serve Mrs Dowson's ice creams with their desserts.

The flavours of real Lancashire interest are Uncle Joe's Mintballs (made with the crushed mintballs made in Wigan), Everton Mint (that was launched at Goodison Park), Cottage Ginger Parkin and Cottage Cookie Crumble (made using ginger confectionary made in Darwen), Pear Drop (using crushed pear drops made in Rawtenstall) and Blackpool Rock. Blackpool Rock ice cream uses crushed real Blackpool rock and is very popular among visitors to the resort (my wife thinks that it tastes a little like crème de menthe frappe ice cream!). In 2006 they launched peanut butter ice cream, the peanut butter being made in Lancashire by KP Foods.

My own tastes are less exotic. Give me the Amaretto and Black Cherry, or the Rum and Raisin, or simply the Vanilla (flavoured, not with vanilla extract or essence, but with real Madagascan vanilla pods). Mrs Dowson's ice creams are a new flavour of Lancashire.

The Roast Beef of Old England

Unless you are a vegetarian, there is nothing quite like a roast beef dinner or a great succulent steak. People argue about which are the best cuts. Roast rib of beef may be best, but is there too much fat in the meat? Is silverside better than topside? Should sirloin ever be roasted? Is a grilled rib-eye as good as a grilled sirloin? Is fillet worth the expense? Personally, I enjoy a piece of brisket, pot-roasted with some good stock and a few chopped vegetables in a very slow/slow oven for three hours, and think that sirloin is far superior to the tasteless fillet, and that with sauces rump steak has the edge.

A Lancastrian's Peppery Steaks

Take some finely chopped onion, garlic and mushrooms and gently cook them in a frying pan in olive oil. Then, when soft, add a tablespoon of freshly ground white peppercorns, stir in and put the pan to one side.

Put your rump steaks under the grill and cook as you like them.

When you turn the steaks over, put the frying pan back on full heat and add a lot of single cream, stir, and when it is almost ready to boil, whip it from the heat and put in your grilled steaks. Turn them over in the creamy, peppery sauce, and serve.

Those of us who like good food also argue about what the beef cow should have been fed on (grass and cereal is the answer) and for how long is should be hanged in a cold store before being butchered. The ideal is three or four weeks. We also argue about what breeds of beef cattle are best. The traditional Lancashire cow was the longhorn, but that is now a 'rare breed'. However it is likely that the county never produced large herds of beef cattle. From the middle of the seventeenth century herds of beef cattle were driven to and through Lancashire from Scotland, and shiploads of cattle fattened in Ireland were shipped from Ireland to Liverpool. Some of the best beef that I eat is in Ireland, and there, it seems, breeds are ignored. Every field on the bogs of Ireland seems to have a motley collection of mongrels accompanied by a bull of no certain strain. Yet they are superb producers of prime beef.

Such discussions would have been as if in a foreign language to most Lancastrians a hundred and more years ago, and to many well into the twentieth century. While better-off Lancashire families enjoyed roast beef for Sunday lunch or a grilled steak on a special occasion, the majority ate only the cheaper cuts. They included minced and diced beef (skirt or shin) that would go in small quantities in stews, pies and hashes (see pages 45–49), and offal.

Tripe

At one time every town in Lancashire had at least one UCP (United Cattle Products) tripe and cow heel shop. Tripe comes from the lining of the cow's stomach and is 'dressed' in the tripe factory before finding itself on the market stall or in a very few butchers' shops. Alas UCP shops are no more. The reason is that Lancastrians are now better off and prefer to eat the formerly more expensive cuts of beef. It is remarkable to think that the first edition of *Ninety-nine ways of Cooking and Serving Dainty Dishes of U.C.P. Tripe and Cow heel*, published by UCP sold 295,000 copies in the late 1940s and 1950s. Tripe, UCP tells us, 'is a cheap food; but it is also a splendid food for the sedentary brain worker, for the invalid, the child, and the nursing mother. While, with its aid, the working man is given a meal tasty and satisfying, economical and strength giving.'

> ❛NINETY NINE WAYS OF COOKING AND SERVING DAINTY DISHES OF UNITED CATTLE PRODUCTS TRIPE AND COW HEEL❜

There are two main sorts of tripe: 'honeycomb' comes from the lining of the cow's second stomach, or reticulum, while 'plain tripe' comes from the cow's first stomach, or rumen. Plain tripe is also known as thick seam or blanket tripe. Many tripe fanatics enjoy dressed tripe just as it comes, eaten cold with salt, pepper and lots of vinegar. Others (and I admit to being among them) cannot take the taste and texture of cold dressed tripe.

Cooked tripe is another matter, and the best tripe for cooking is honeycomb tripe.

Tripe and Onions
This is the Number One Lancashire tripe dish.

Wash 1¼ lb honeycomb tripe and then put in a pan of cold water. Bring to the boil. Then drain, rinse in cold water and cut the meat into two-inch squares.

Chop three large onions and put them with the tripe, a couple of bay leaves and a pint of full cream milk into a saucepan. Bring to the boil and simmer gently until very tender (about two hours). Remove the bay leaves. Blend in an ounce of butter and add to the saucepan, stirring while heating so that it thickens the milk. Add some finely chopped parsley and some freshly ground nutmeg.

This is ready to eat, but you can go one better: pour the contents of the saucepan into a dish, sprinkle the top with a layer of good

Lancashire cheese, and put under the grill until the cheese is melted.

Eat this with good bread, toast or mashed potatoes.

Tripe with Dumplings

Dice one pound of honeycomb tripe and four large potatoes, and slice finely two large onions. Put them into a large pan with 1½ ounces of bacon fat, one pint of water and salt and pepper to taste. Bring to the boil and simmer for 1–1½ hours.

Make some dumplings from four ounces of flour, two ounces of suet, half a teaspoon of baking powder, a pinch of salt and water to mix. Put these into the stew and cook for an extra 20–30 minutes.

Note: for those who consider tripe a 'peasant food' and not worth eating, it is worth remembering that, in French gastronomic circles, *Tripe a la Mode de Caen, Tripe a la Napolitaine* and *Tripe en Casserole* are highly rated dishes even today.

Cow Heel

Cow heel is a great source of gelatine when cooked slowly for a long time. It can therefore be added to soups and stews to add a rich, thick texture. It is usually available on market stalls and in some butchers' shops, usually in old industrial towns, ready for use.

Cow Heel and Beef Stew

Put a cow heel (split in half by the butcher) and one pound of shin beef into a large pan. Stick four cloves into two large, peeled onions, and put them in the pan. Pour in two pints of good beef stock, put a lid on the pan, bring to the boil and simmer for three hours.

Take the cow heel, meat and onions from the stock. Chop the meat and onions (discarding the cloves) and remove the meat from the cow heel. Put back into the pan of stock, re-heat and serve.

Cow heel consists of the white ligaments and tendons around the heel bones of the cow. When cooked very slowly, with shin beef, they release lots of flavour and gelatine that produces a thick, delicious gravy.

Roger and Bernie
Webster and their
farm shop.

Notes:

1. This stew has often been used in a cow heel and steak pie. Line a dish with short crust pastry, spoon in meats and onion with only a little stock (the rest can be used in a beef soup). Put on a pastry lid and bake in a moderate oven for 45 minutes.

2. Put some dumplings into the pan and simmer for 20 minutes before serving.

Quality and the Farm Shop

Roger and Bernie Webster of Taylor's Farm have a mixed farm near Lathom in the Lancashire lowlands. In 2003 income from the farm was falling and expenditure rising, so they, like so many farmers in the county, decided to cut out the middlemen and open a farm shop in which they could sell their produce straight to the public. At first their shop opened only on Friday afternoon and Saturday, but by April

2006 demand was so great that they extended opening to four days – Wednesdays to Saturdays.

The basic product of their shop is their home-reared beef. The majority of the feed eaten by their cattle is grown on the farm, including the pasture over which the cows can wander and graze freely. The cattle are slaughtered as near to 24 months as possible. If they were kept beyond 24 months then EU regulations insist that the spinal column be removed and BSE tests made. This is very expensive. The carcasses are then hung in cold store for three weeks to enhance taste and tenderness.

Lamb, pork and chickens are bought in for their shop, all from farms in the region where animal welfare and husbandry are a top priority. The farms on which each animal that they sell was reared is known and records are at hand. Bernie once asked a local supermarket to source some of the prime beef that they were selling; it took them over six months.

'By cutting out the middleman,' Roger explained, 'we increase our income but at the same time can cut back on costs to the consumer. We aim to produce better quality of meat than the supermarket at a competitive price. We are aiming for quality and price; especially quality.'

There are several other similar ventures throughout Lancashire where farmers are trying to sell beef, lamb, pork and poultry that is superior in quality to what most supermarkets offer. The Websters draw their customers from up to 25 miles away to stock up for their freezers. One customer was going to visit her daughter in South Africa. She took a case of Taylor's Farm beef, simply because her daughter complained that 'I can't get meat of that quality here!'

Lancashire Broth

Len Pitchford was a butcher at Culcheth and he prided himself on the quality of the beef cattle (and sheep) that he bought at the market every Monday, then sent to the abattoir, butchered and sold in his shop. One day a newly married woman went into his shop and said, 'Mr Pitchford. My husband keeps going on about the oxtail that his mother cooked for him. Have you an oxtail that I can cook and surprise him with?'

Len said that he hadn't, but that the following Tuesday he would have the perfect oxtail waiting for her. The following Tuesday she called and Len sold her an oxtail that he had cut into nice chunks.

She returned the next day. 'That oxtail was horrid,' she complained. 'It was inedible!'

'But it came from a perfect beef cow,' protested Len. 'It was spot on two years old. It won a silver medal at the Liverpool show! It had been hung for over three weeks. You can't get better Hereford beef!'

'Well, we tried to eat it, but it was horrible and tough!'

'How did you cook it?'

'Why, I grilled it.'

Oxtail was once highly prized, but is now grossly underrated and underused. Rarely do you see it in supermarkets (Booths being an exception: I once bought a splendid oxtail in their Ulverston branch). The point about oxtail is that it must be cooked very slowly, in plenty of water (or stock), hence oxtail soup. The following is a rich broth using oxtail and that other cut, shin beef, which must be cooked slowly.

Take 1½lb finely chopped shin beef, including sinews and other tough bits, and an oxtail cut into short sections. Put them in a large pan with four pints of cold water. Bring to the boil, and then simmer gently for three hours.

Add as wide a variety of chopped vegetables are you want or can: e.g. a large onion, a leek, a potato, a couple of carrots, a couple of turnips or half a swede, a small parsnip, a handful of dried beans or peas that have previously been soaked in cold water for twelve hours, a piece of savoy cabbage etc. As in most old traditional dishes, there are lots of opinions as to what should go in and what should not! Add also three tablespoonfuls of pearl barley, perhaps a few red lentils if you have some, some mixed herbs and salt and pepper. Bring back to the simmer for another hour.

Twenty minutes before the end of cooking you could pop in some suet dumplings (turn up the heat a little so that the pan is just boiling and cover) or serve with good wholemeal bread.

WAKES WEEK FOOD

ACCORDING TO THE OXFORD DICTIONARY the term 'wake', indicating a holiday, comes from a 'rule of the Early Church that certain feast-days should be preceded by services lasting through the night. When this rule had ceased to exist, the vigil continued to be the pretext for nocturnal festivity, and thence the word *wake* was extended to denote not only the eve but also the feast-day itself, and the whole period during which festivities continued.'

In other words, it was an excuse to have a great old party. And that pious virgin Queen Elizabeth I so disliked her subjects enjoying a good old blowout that she abolished wakes. James I reinstated them, but the idea of wakes disappeared other than in two contexts. The first was a party to commemorate a recently departed well-loved friend or relation. The second is the Wakes Week, the week-long (later fortnight) summer holiday enjoyed by the working classes of Lancashire and the West Riding.

When wakes weeks were at their height, some Lancashire towns almost closed down for the duration. Well into the 1970s, during Preston's two wakes weeks, even newsagents and the corner shops closed, and on the middle Saturday the town's two main thoroughfares, Fishergate and Friargate, were almost deserted. Every factory and mill in a town closed for wakes weeks, and this gave the management the opportunity to arrange to have the main boiler descaled and other annual maintenance carried out. Different towns had different wakes weeks so that the seaside towns could cope. For instance, Bolton's wakes weeks were always the last two full weeks of June, whereas Preston's were the first full two weeks of July.

Wakes Weeks were usually confined to local holiday towns such as Blackpool and Morecambe, but this group of young mill workers from Lancashire headed south in 1914 to Ilfracombe in Devon. Little did the men know, but months later they would be in the trenches, fighting in the First World War.

I remember in 1962 my family going for the Preston fortnight to stay in a caravan at Bude in Cornwall. Father then worked in the aircraft factory on Strand Road in Preston and it was the first time we had ventured so far. These were pre-motorway days and the route from Preston went through the centres of places like Wigan and Warrington, Worcester and Gloucester, and crossed the suspension bridge at Bristol. We travelled overnight and pulled into a lay-by just after Bristol where we cooked breakfast on a primus-stove. Several other families were doing the same; they all had Preston accents, and the breadwinner of one also worked on Strand Road. 'Small world,' he said.

The idea of a wakes week is rapidly vanishing. The mills and factories no longer dominate employment in the county. The most popular resorts like Blackpool and Morecambe are now day trips by car. And two or three weeks can be spent far away from home where sunshine is guaranteed, at any time of the year, provided that you have 'booked your holidays with work'.

Few working Lancashire families up to the late 1950s or 1960s had a car, so they travelled to and from their holiday by bus or train. Proper hotels were too expensive. After the Second World War Billy Butlin established his famous holiday camps and other entrepreneurs bought coastal fields at places like Rhyl and around Morecambe Bay, covering them with caravans that could be hired by the week. Yet the archetypal wakes week was always held 'in digs'. There each family had one or two bedrooms, shared use of the bathroom and ate in the communal dining room. Large boarding houses could house several families, and dominating the scene was the landlady, who would impose rules like, 'Everyone must be out by ten, and must not return before five-thirty,' 'Please give 24 hours notice if you want to run a bath,' and 'Do not bring sand into the house.'

'PLEASE GIVE 24 HOURS NOTICE IF YOU WANT TO RUN A BATH'

The fascinating point by today's standards is the way food was organised in the wakes week boarding house. The landlady did not provide the sort of set breakfast we see everywhere today: fruit juice, grapefuit or cereal, followed the eggs and bacon, toast and marmalade and tea or coffee. Or that sort of thing. Each family bought the food that it wanted and she cooked it for them.

So at the start of the week you would buy tea, sugar, cornflakes, butter, cooking fat, eggs, bacon and so on. The basics. And every morning you would pop out to the nearest grocers or butcher and buy the food needed that evening and top up things that were getting low, such as bread and milk. Then, come six-thirty, the landlady would serve you the soup, then the main course and then the pudding (that is, of course, if you wanted three courses) using the ingredients

Walking Day
This is in Leigh,
Lancashire,
c. 1955.

that you had purchased and that she kept in your cupboard in the dining room. Other families staying in the same digs had their own cupboards and they bought what they wanted to eat. So the poor landlady, who was often pictured as being a bit of an ogress, would have to prepare several different meals every evening as well, when cooked breakfasts were ordered, several lots of egg and bacon sourced from each family's cupboard in the morning.

Needless to say, the poor woman sometimes got it wrong. She might accidentally use the Smith's tea leaves to make a pot of tea for the Jones family. And then the Smith family might notice how the level of tea leaves in their caddy had fallen when they hadn't drunk any tea. So the Smith family would assume that the landlady was stealing their tea!

Life for the holidaymaker could be made easier by ordering their supplies in advance. For instance, in the 1920s one Lancashire firm of grocers, James Duckworth Ltd., advertised in local papers just before the town's wakes weeks. 'If you are visiting the Blackpool or St.Annes District, leave your grocery and provision order at any of our branches,' said their advert, and 'Goods [will be] delivered at your Apartments to await your arrival.'

The two things that people going away did not want to buy were salt and pepper. Why waste money on a big tub of salt and a shaker of pepper? Most of it would be wasted! So the landlady provided the salt and pepper and would advertise the fact by stating, 'Use of cruet extra!'

In 1938 one Bolton couple went on honeymoon to Blackpool. They had been too much in love to read the advert for their boarding house properly, so they missed the bit about 'Use of cruet extra.' Through the week they budgeted carefully so that they would have just enough cash to pay their bill before they caught the train back home. But when the bill arrived there was the extra ... 'Use of cruet – 2/6'. Two shilling and six pence (half a crown or 25p in today's money) was a lot of money in those days. In fact, they might have had good cause to accuse the landlady of extortion. They did not have a spare 2/6. So they had to sign a witnessed IOU and send the landlady a postal order on their return!

WALKING DAY

One of the social highlights of the Lancashire year used to be the Walking Day, when the congregation of each church, headed by a brass band, processed around their parish, with banners showing scenes from the Bible or the life of some saint. In Kirkham the event was ecumenical, for all the churches joined together on Walking Day and perambulated the entire town. In larger towns each church did its own thing. The most contentious were the Bible-thumping churches, whose processions stopped at regular intervals (often close to the doors of public houses) when the minister would harangue those watching on the wages of sin and the folly of their ways. Often drinkers would stream out of the pub that was being targeted and heckle the preacher! Great fun was had by all and such walking days continued well into the 1960s, and even 1970s.

There were other similar events. Miners' Gala days, Open Days, November fetes and the like. All included some form of refreshment and the tea urn or several huge brown enamel teapots were constantly full. No coffee here, and certainly no booze! Children were supplied with plastic cups of weak orange squash.

The solid part of the refreshment was sometimes a help-yourself buffet or, more likely (for many would help themselves too generously), a paper plate on which each participant's food was laid out. There would be a cold sausage roll, half a whist pie, and bread rolls cut in half lengthways bearing a helping of egg and cress, meat paste, and boiled ham. Cakes figured prominently: maids of honour, ice buns, jam tarts and so on.

Perhaps many of the problems now afflicting Lancashire society (especially urban ones) are caused by the lack of a sense of community of the kind that was engendered by such old-fashioned events?

POULTRY AND EGGS

BEFORE THE INDUSTRIAL REVOLUTION, when the Lancashire population was largely rural, most families might have had a few chickens and perhaps a duck or two, or a pair of geese scratching a living outside the cottage door. Through the spring and summer the hens would produce eggs, though in winter egg production would stop. A cockerel would run with the hens and some of the eggs would be incubated. Some of the resulting chickens would go to next year's flock; the rest, as well as those past the egg-laying stage, would go in the pot. And the main feast day of the year, Christmas, was tradition-ally celebrated not with a turkey (an import from the United States of America) but with a goose.

Most families who went to live in the growing mill towns could no longer keep their own poultry, so eggs had to be purchased from the meagre income and eating chicken became a special treat.

Hens' eggs were, of course, in great demand because they were often an essential ingredient in making the puddings and cakes so enjoyed by Lancastrians in the late nineteenth and through most of the twentieth centuries. So the battery method of producing vast numbers of eggs at minimum cost was developed. Battery sheds were set up containing hundreds of small cages in three tiers, and in each cage were stuffed three hens. They were provided with food and water, and to stop them 'going off the lay' in autumn, electric lights were switched on at night to fool their hormones that it was still summer. There was a problem in that the three hens in a tiny cage would get bored and start to peck at each other. The solution was straightforward. The battery hens were de-beaked, a third of the upper beak being burnt off with a special tool. Then special breeds of battery hens were produced. When they started to lay on day one the farmer would know to within a day or two when they all would stop laying. He could then slaughter the lot and next day bring in a new lot of hens. It was all an economic miracle.

It was then discovered that it was possible to produce breeds of hens that would convert a high proportion of their food intake into meat very quickly and that had less bone and other waste in the carcass. Thousands were – and still are – packed into sheds where they have just enough room to turn round. There they feed and grow. After a few days many may be killed to produce the poussin that we see in the supermarkets, hyped up by the well-advertised 'delicious spatch-cocked chicken'. Those raising the chickens know precisely what day all the birds in their shed will weight 2½ pounds and 3½ pounds, the size wanted by the retailers, because growth is so constant in these genetically selected birds. And those poor birds are what we see sold as plain 'chicken'. It's cheap. It's full of protein (and antibiotics).

Free range chickens are happy chickens sheltering from the rain in this photograph.

It's convenient. But look carefully at the legs of the chicken. Often they are not strong enough to stand upright, so they crouch with their yellow legs touching the litter that is fouled by their droppings. And there on the legs are the brown or black burns caused by contact with the acrid droppings.

Such eggs and chickens have no place among the flavours of Lancashire. You can buy, at farms, farmers' markets and even in the better supermarkets, free-range eggs and chickens that have spent their short but happy lives wandering around in the sunshine.

They may cost a little more, but they are humanely cared for and taste far better.

EGGS CHOPPED UP IN A CUP

Take a couple of boiled eggs, shell while hot and chop finely with a little butter, salt and pepper. Put this into a cup and eat with a teaspoon.

This was a Lancashire cure for all sorts of fairly minor ailments, from the common cold to influenza.

Hindle Wakes

Hindle wakes is a corruption of 'hen of the wake', the chicken that would be eaten on a wake or feast day (see page 96). Then the chicken would not be the young, fat and tender chicken that we enjoy today, but a scrawny old hen or cock that would take several hours of slow cooking before it was tender. This is a very old Lancashire dish.

First of all find a large free-range chicken, ideally in the four- to six-pound size bracket. A good farm shop or farmers' market should be able to provide one.

Soak a pound of dried prunes in water (or, preferably, cold tea) for twelve hours. De-stone and chop up the prunes and mix with four ounces of breadcrumbs, a finely chopped onion, salt and pepper, and some finely chopped parsley, sage and thyme. Moisten this stuffing with lemon juice and then stuff the neck of the bird and (loosely) the body cavity of the bird. Stitch up the opening at the rear of the bird to prevent the stuffing there escaping. Put the chicken into a large pan and cover with cold water. Add a glass of white wine, a chopped onion and seasoning. Bring to the boil and then gently simmer until the bird is tender. That will be about three hours for a large young chicken, but may take a little longer if the bird has been building up its legs muscles and sinews by wandering wherever it wanted. Leave the bird in the liquid to go cold.

Melt an ounce of butter in a saucepan and stir in half an ounce of plain flour. Cook for one minute, stirring continually. Then add cold stock from the pan a little at a time, heating and stirring continually until you have a creamy sauce. Into that squeeze the juice of one lemon. Cover the surface of the sauce with greaseproof paper or the paper from around a pound of butter (this prevents a skin forming on the sauce) and let the sauce cool.

Serve the chicken coated with sauce, and the stuffing in a separate dish. This goes well with a segment of lemon, new potatoes and a green salad.

The Perfect Free-Range Chicken

Take a chicken weighing about three pounds and slip your fingers between the skin and meat at the neck end of the breast. Push your fingers further so that there is a gap between the breast meat and skin. Remove your fingers and slide between meat and skin several quarter-inch slabs of butter (cut them from a block of butter taken from the fridge).

Take two oranges and peel the zest from them. Place the chicken in a roasting tin on the orange zest and some fresh sprigs of thyme and parsley, and roast in a moderately hot oven for ten minutes before turning the oven down to moderate. Cooking time is about half an hour per pound of bird, but check by sticking the point of a knife into the base of the thighs. When the juices run clear the bird is cooked; if they are pink with blood put the chicken back in the oven.

After about three quarters of an hour of the cooking time, start to baste the chicken with the melted butter and juices in the pan every quarter of an hour until the bird is cooked.

Serve the chicken with the herby, orangey, buttery contents of the roasting tin as a sauce.

What to eat for Christmas dinner?

A free-range hen explores beyond the farm fence.

At one time a chicken or a capon would have satisfied most families, but chicken is too much of an everyday meat for most people today. So now most buy a turkey. Most turkeys are raised rather like the poor little broiler chickens I described earlier, so if you want ordinary turkey buy it from a farm that makes good husbandry a priority.

Even so, ordinary turkey has become very commonplace. You can even buy sliced turkey breast the year round in delicatessens. Far better, if you want turkey, to go for a free-range bronze turkey that, though much more expensive, has a far more special flavour and moist texture.

However, the traditional Lancashire Christmas fare is not the American turkey but the farmyard goose, and here in the county Lancashire Geese produces more free-range Christmas geese than anyone else in England.

I visited Norman Lea, who runs the goose farm by the Ormskirk–Southport road in early May, when his breeding herd of around one thousand geese were just starting to lay their eggs. As I arrived I could see the white geese scattered across a huge field,

'A GOOSE AT MICHAELMAS WAS ONCE A POPULAR DISH'

Norman Lea.

Lancashire geese.

nibbling grass. But when I went to the field gate to take a photograph of them the geese stopped nibbling grass and slowly began to process to some large sheds at the top of the field.

'I only go to this gate in the evening,' explained Norman. 'They know that it's bedtime and that they will get some corn before they go to sleep. Then I lock them in until the morning. We have confused them and they think that it must be time for bed simply because we are here!'

And I thought that geese were intelligent birds!

The eggs laid by the breeding stock hatch in June and feed on grass by day in the fields and a good helping of wheat in their sheds just before nightfall. The first geese could be killed and prepared for cooking in September (a goose at Michaelmas was once a popular dish) but today the market demands goose for Christmas or New Year and very rarely any other time of the year. Six to eight weeks before Christmas Norman increases the wheat ration and hopes that the weather in late November and December will be very cold so that the geese will lay down big fat deposits. In very mild winters the geese

remain very lean, for it takes frost before they lay down upwards of a kilogram of fat.

Fourteen days before Christmas the geese are killed and hung to tenderise and develop a full flavour. They are then plucked and dressed.

Up to a few years ago Lancashire Geese produced around 30,000 geese, but today the output is closer to 10,000. And most are eaten in the Christmas–New Year festive season.

Roasting the Christmas goose

> First cut off the legs at the base of the thighs and put them away in the fridge.
>
> Next, prepare the Apple and Prune Stuffing. Take the flesh from a dozen prunes that have been soaked in water overnight and chop it up. Take a medium onion and a large cooking apple (preferably NOT a bramley, but one that does not fall; you might use a couple of Egremont russets instead) and chop them up. Mix apple, onion, prunes, some chopped sage, thyme and parsley with about 6 oz of fresh breadcrumbs and season with salt and pepper. Put this stuffing in the cavity of the goose and sew up to prevent the stuffing leaking out.
>
> Roast the goose in a slow oven for half an hour per pound, at regular but short periods taking it from the oven and draining away the fat from the roasting tin.
>
> This fat can be put into jars and used to make the most superb roast potatoes. Some will be used to cook the legs …

Making confit of goose legs

On Boxing Day morning, cut each leg into two (drumstick and thigh) and cover with plenty of salt. Leave for six hours.

Wipe away the salt, put the legs into a deep ovenproof container (earthenware by tradition, but I find a small casserole ideal) and cover with fat from your goose. Put in a very slow oven for about three hours, then allow to cool.

You can store the confit in a cool pantry for some time (I have kept it up to the end of March). Take the legs from the fat and wipe. Heat thoroughly in a frying pan. Remove the meat from the bone and enjoy! It is especially good eaten like the Chinese crispy duck, on rice pancakes, with hoisin sauce, and cucumber and spring onion.

If you roast the goose with the legs on, the legs usually end up dried out and inedible. Confit makes them deliciously tender and when we eat it, it evokes memories of the Christmas past.

FISH

'Shrympes. Take shrympes, and set hem in water and a litull salt, and lete hem boile ones or a litull more. And serue hem, for the colde; And no maner sauce but vinegre.'

Harliean Manuscript, 4016., c.1300.

IT IS NOT SURPRISING THAT, being a coastal county with the broad shallow estuaries of the Mersey, Ribble, Wyre, Lune and Morecambe Bay, and a countryside that was – until massive drainage took place from the eighteenth century – a maze of lakes as well rivers and streams, fish and shellfish have long been important in the Lancashire diet.

In bygone days Lancashire fisheries were privately owned and jealously protected. For instance, in the twelfth century on the River Wyre, the fishing rights at Rawcliffe were owned by William of Lancaster who rented them to a knight called William of Carlton for six pence per annum. Six pence was a fair old price in those days. Later, from 1205 onwards, various landowners granted stretches of the Wyre between St Michael's and the sea to the monks of Cockersand Abbey. Both landowners and monks benefited from the grant. The monks could catch fish there and

A brace of sea trout from the River Hodder, caught on fly in the dead of a summer's night. For many, sea trout (also called salmon-trout) has a far better flavour than salmon.

Flounder, or fluke. Once the most popular fish in Lancashire.

eat them on the many days when they couldn't eat red meat, and the landowners' souls had a better chance of reaching heaven.

After Cockersand Abbey was dissolved by Henry VIII all the rights of fishing (mainly for salmon, sea trout, flounders and eels) went back into private hands with much wrangling as to who owned what and where. For example, in 1567 William Burroe of Larbreck had twenty acres of saltmarsh by the Wyre estuary at Thornton and the fishing rights in the river beyond the saltmarsh. Or so he said! The court records of Elizabeth I in 1568 tell how, on 20 August 1567, Henry Butler argued that he had the fishing rights there and so, 'with six riotous persons … with force of arms … [he, Butler] had entered on the marshland and taken his [Burroe's] nets out of the river and refused to give them back.'

A few years later, in 1580, William Kirkby built a weir across the Wyre just downstream of St Michael's. All the fishery owners on the river complained to the Duchy Court and a Crown Enquiry was convened. The outcome was that the weir was pulled down.

Similar cases occurred throughout Lancashire on rivers and lakes between the twelfth and sixteenth centuries.

Even on what we consider to be the open shore, fishing was not free for all. In the seventeenth and eighteenth centuries, for example, the shore between what is now Southport and Ainsdale was divided up into 'stalls' or fairly short lengths. The Lord of the Manor rented each of these stalls to individual fishermen. They set long stake-nets along the beach close to the low water mark, and when the tide had receded they went along and gathered the fish that had been trapped by the nets. As late as 1855 cases were being brought to court over the rights to fish the beaches here.

Fluke Hall named after the flounder.

There are two reasons why fisheries were so important and so keenly guarded. The first was that the Catholic Church prohibited the eating of red meat on about one third of days, the Days of Obligation. Fish could be eaten on these days (see also page 2). Even today, perhaps more than in any other English county – for Lancashire has always had a higher proportion of Catholics in its population than any other county – Lancastrians often keep this tradition of not eating meat and flesh on Fridays … and especially on Good Fridays. In medieval times, when the church was perhaps at its most dominant, several species of freshwater fish were introduced to the county to supplement those naturally occurring here, for instance pike, carp, bream and grayling.

The second reason why fish were so important was that, until transport allowed for the rapid movement of animals from other parts of the country, protein was scarce in the diet of the ordinary folk, especially in winter and spring. In inshore waters, nutritious fish like whiting, cod, dabs and flounders (called *flukes* in Lancashire, hence Fluke Hall near Pilling) were abundant, whilst the once very numerous salmon entered the rivers in spring and was netted in huge numbers. On 31 March 1732 3,190 salmon were taken in one sweep of the net on the Ribble at Penwortham. Most if not all of them would have been carried up Fishergate (the fishers' street) to Preston Market. This was valuable protein at a time when the salted pork supply was running low.

Today most people would turn up their noses at eating eels, called snigs in Lancashire or pike (though both are excellent when properly prepared). In 1712 they were much in demand.

In his diary entry for 21st June 1712 Nicholas Blundell tells us that, 'I took 31 Pickarills [small pike] in my Snigary [pool for catching eels].' On the 22nd 'William Ainsworth went with me both in the Morning & Night to my Snigary, in the Morning I got 10 Picks [pike] & about 9 Pound of Eles, & at night I got 21 Picks.' In the morning of the 23rd William Ainsworh again helped Blundell take '55 Piks & about 3½ lb. of Eles … Henry Stananaught went in the after noone with me to my Snigary, we tool 10 Piks …'

All the eels and pike went to market and where sold to be cooked for the table.

Besides fresh fish huge quantities of salted herrings from northeast England and dried herrings from Scotland were imported into Lancashire to provide protein for those who could afford to buy them. The Crown granted pontage rights (the right to exact tolls for crossing) for Edisford Bridge to the town of Clitheroe. The tolls were to fund repairs to the bridge. In 1339 the toll for carrying barrels containing 1000 herrings over the Ribble at Edisford was a ha'penny. There seems to have been more profit in fresh sea fish, for the toll for taking a cartload of sea fish over the bridge was four pence. Incidentally, if you go to Edisford, look under the present bridge and you will see some large stone blocks in the river that were part of the ancient bridge.

Up to the second half of the twentieth century fresh fish was inexpensive, for trawlers from Fleetwood returned from around the seas of Iceland and Norway laden, and inshore fishing boats from Southport, Lytham, Sunderland Point and Morecambe took a fine harvest of fish from coastal waters. The Cod War of 1976 with Iceland signalled the end of deep-water trawlers; the end came with the United Nations Convention on the Law of the Sea, which led to Iceland and Norway closing their high seas fisheries to other countries. Meanwhile, the European Union's appalling fisheries policy [sic] has seen the collapse of our inshore fish stocks.

THE FISH-AND-CHIP SHOP

While the first potato chips were fried in France in about 1775, in England fried chips were not commercially prepared until about 1830, initially in Oldham. In 1870 Faulkner & Co. of Oldham began to make frying ranges and this encouraged people to open fish-and-chip shops, selling fried hake and cod with chips, in every town and large village. The fish were mostly landed at Fleetwood and transported by the expanding rail network.

Fifty years ago 'chippies' sold mainly fish and chips, together with pies and mushy peas. Today, with fish being so much more expensive, pie, pudding or curry are far more popular accompaniments with the fried chips.

If you want a change from the usual sorts of fish, or fish fried or grilled in the same old way, try these Lancashire recipes.

Fish Pie

Take a fillet or steak of three quite different sorts of fish, for example cod, salmon and smoked haddock. Cook each for about five minutes in a pan of simmering water. Remove any skin and bones, and break the fish into bite-sized pieces.

Put the fish at the bottom of a casserole dish and pour over parsley sauce (to which you might add four ounces of peeled prawns). Add some butter, salt and milk to some boiled potatoes and mash well. Spoon these potatoes over the fish, grate some Lancashire cheese over the top and put under a hot grill until the top is nice and brown.

Some markets sell smaller fillets or off-cuts for much less than the neater, larger fillets or steaks. They are ideal for this dish.

Fish Cakes

You can use just about any inexpensive fish in this recipe, such as grey mullet (they abound in our estuaries in summer), flounders (ditto), mackerel, whiting, dabs, pike or rainbow trout, or cheap cuts or bargain offers from the market. Cook the fish by either boiling or baking in kitchen foil in the oven. Then remove every bone and scrap of skin and break into flakes.

> Mix the flaked fish with an equal volume of mashed potato. Add some finely chopped curly parsley and season with salt and pepper.

> Mould into cakes. Brush well with beaten egg and then dip into breadcrumbs before frying until they are well browned on both sides.

Baked trout, Sea Trout, Salmon or Sea-bass

Lancashire has some of the best fishing in Britain for these four fish in the Ribble and Lune and their estuaries. What follows is the easiest, cleanest and, because the fish is sealed away so that no flavour can escape, tastiest way of cooking these. If you do not know a generous angler, you can buy these in your nearest fish market.

A fresh salmon taken in a net in the Ribble estuary. Professional, licensed salmon netsmen are a dying breed.

Take the fish, clean and wash well, and place in the centre of a large piece of kitchen foil. Obviously, with large salmon use a piece of the fish, though the smaller 'grilse', weighing four or five pounds, can be cooked whole.

Put some butter mixed with chopped dill, thyme and parsley (use dried mixed herbs if you have no fresh) in the body cavity, and put a few small pieces of butter onto the top of the fish. Sprinkle over a little salt and some freshly ground black pepper …

Wrap the kitchen foil around the fish to make a well-sealed parcel.

Bake in a moderately hot oven until well cooked (about half an hour for a trout or bass weighing three pounds). Alternatively put on the barbeque (a 3 lb sea trout fresh from the Lune and barbequed on the riverbank took only fifteen minutes. It was delicious!).

Salmon Paste

This recipe was found written on a scrap of paper in an old note-book of recipes belonging to Elizabeth Davies and comes from the Wigan area. It is possible that the salmon used in this dish was tinned salmon, though fresh salmon from the Ribble or Lune are equally likely.

Remove all skin and bones from a large piece of poached fresh salmon or from a large tin of salmon. Chop up as finely as possible. Take two slices of white bread for every pound of salmon. Crumble the bread and mix with the salmon. Season with salt and pepper. Press into a mould (such as a small bowl or basin) and pour melted butter over the top. Put in a cool place and eat on sandwiches or with salad.

Today we would put the salmon, bread and seasoning in the food processor and blitz it to a fine paste before putting the paste into a mould.

John and
Michael Price
and their
smokehouse.

THE PORT OF LANCASTER SMOKEHOUSE

I first met John Price in 1993 when I had caught a couple of salmon that I wanted smoked for Christmas. 'Tell me how you like it smoked' he said, and gave me a small taste of three he had just smoked. I preferred the strongest flavour. 'Fine,' he said. 'That's how they will be smoked.'

Then John's was a small business, mainly processing the wild salmon caught on the Lune and Ribble estuaries. Today, with his son Michael, John has made the Port of Lancaster Smokehouse one of the greatest shrines to gastronomy in not only Lancashire but also all Britain.

Here you can buy smoked wild salmon as well as farmed salmon (Michael sources only the best), smoked trout, smoked mackerel, smoked haddock (superb, poached, for breakfast with a poached egg), smoked kippers (the Smokehouse's own kippers are the most succulent I have ever tasted) and smoked eel. The Prices also now smoke several meats, including duck and goose breasts (see below), chicken breasts, bacon and Lancashire sausages. In season their shop at Glasson Dock on the Lune estuary is a good source of oven-ready game: hare, partridge, pheasant, venison, mallard and, sometimes if you are lucky, teal and woodcock.

The shop also stocks local top quality foods like Mrs Kirkham's cheese (see page 87) and Morecambe Bay shrimps.

If you can't visit the shop, then you may encounter Michael with his mobile stall at many of the farmers' markets in the county.

SMOKED DUCK OR GOOSE BREAST

Lightly oil a heavy frying pan, put on the stove and when hot put in duck or goose breasts, meat side down. (For a light lunch one breast will feed two, but for dinner you need one per person.)

Leave them meat-side down for about thirty seconds, then turn them over with the skin-side down. Turn down the heat and let them warm through thoroughly. This will take five or ten minutes, but the thick skin will prevent burning.

Drain away all fat, or mop it up with kitchen paper. Then add an extra flavour. This might be destoned cherries, or a dollop of Cumberland or cranberry sauce. I find home-made crab apple jelly perfect for this dish (see page 67). Serve with a green salad and new potatoes.

Eel Pie

Make some stuffing by mixing the finely grated zest and juice of two lemons with eight ounces of fresh, dry breadcrumbs, two finely chopped shallots (or a small onion), and some chopped curly parsley and salt and pepper. Put this in the bottom of an ovenproof dish.

Clean and wash two pounds of eels, cut them up into two-inch chunks and put the pale (under) side down on the stuffing so that the cut part of the eel chunks is in contact with the stuffing. Put a few knobs of butter over the eels.

Put a short-crust pastry lid over the top and cook in a moderately hot oven for fifteen minutes, then turn the temperature down to slow/moderate until the pastry is well browned.

Smoked Eel Pâté

Eel pie is an old flavour of Lancashire; this is a new one. The basic ingredient comes from the Port of Lancaster Smokehouse for I have not found another source of smoked eel in the county.

Take some smoked eel fillets, break them into small pieces, checking that there are no bones, and place in the food processor. Add the juice of one lemon and the finely grated zest of half a lemon for every two pieces of eel fillet. Season with a little salt and plenty of freshly ground black pepper.

Blitz with the food processor until you have a fine paste. Now, with the food processor still running, pour in a tablespoonful of melted clarified butter for every two pieces of fillet.

When thoroughly mixed, put the pâté into a small bowl and chill.

Serve with hot toast.

I know that the thought of eating eel will not appeal to most modern Lancastrians but, believe me, it is delicious. I once had two friends round for dinner who fish the Lune and Ribble. I asked them what fish they thought they were eating: they guessed at trout, grayling, chub, dace, pike ... but not eel!

Shrimps

Shrimps are still fairly abundant in the Ribble Estuary and Morecambe Bay and every day you can watch boats heading out from Morecambe or Lytham, or tractors from Southport to harvest them. The shrimps are grey-brown when caught and only get their pink coloration when boiled.

Peeling the shrimps is the worst job there is if you have not done it often before.

Peter Rimmer from Marshside comes from a shrimping family and has been a shrimper all his life. When he was eight years old his mother started him off by teaching him to peel shrimps. At first he had to peel half a pint every day before he went to school, and the better he got the more he had to peel.

Before he retired (though he still goes out in his old shrimping tractor when the weather is kind) he fished the two five-hour, low-water periods every day and night, Monday to Saturday mornings, and in the seven-hour slots separating these fishing times he boiled his catch in a copper boiler, ate and tried to catch up on his sleep. Meanwhile his wife and two other women peeled the shrimps he had caught and boiled. This was their lifestyle for over forty years, week in and week out.

Recently I joined Peter and went with him on his tractor miles out in the Ribble estuary. When we got back he have me a couple of pints of live shrimps. It took me almost two hours to peel them ... and there were just enough to make a starter for two! So buy Southport or Morecambe Bay shrimps already potted in butter and enjoy

Three miles out in the estuary, Peter sets up his trawl.

Separating the shrimps from the crabs, flounder fry, sand-eels and bits of seaweed.

An advert for Southport shrimps.

them with hot toast. Delicious! One of the greatest flavours of Lancashire!

A tip: Put the plastic pot containing the shrimps in the microwave for 10–15 seconds before serving. That will soften the butter and helps enhance the flavour.

Cockles

These can be gathered from cocklebanks out in the Ribble estuary or Morecambe Bay *provided that they are open*. When stocks are low the local authorities declare the banks closed and it is then illegal to take cockles from them. Note, however, that the cockle beds are often far from dry land and, as a fairly recent incident demonstrated on Morecambe Bay, they are dangerous. So it is better to buy your cockles from the local markets.

You need at least a pint of cockles per person. Give them a good wash under the running cold tap, discarding any that are open. Then drop them into a large pan of salted boiling water and leave then there until they have all opened. This will take only a few minutes. Drain, put into bowls and serve with wholemeal bread and butter.

Great Lancashire food!

Note: you could cook some cockles and put them into a fish pie (see page 111).

Mussels

Mussels *should not* be gathered on the Lancashire coast, taken home, boiled and eaten. They will certainly carry bacteria that will, to put it mildly, make you ill. The mussels that you can buy in our markets will have been grown off the coast of Ireland, Wales or the west of Scotland and been cleansed in sterile water. Like the farmed oysters we can also buy, they are delicious, but not really a Lancashire delicacy.

With a trawler to Iceland

Ray Ball is now a netsman for salmon on the Ribble estuary, but when he left school he signed on as a hand on a Fleetwood trawler set for Icelandic waters in the years before the Cod War. I asked him what a trip on a trawler was like.

Wyre Victory, the fleetwood trawler in which Ray (bottom left) 'looked up'!

'It took three days steaming to get to Iceland and for the entire journey the ship rolled and pitched in the Atlantic waves. The three days back were even worse, for then the ship was heavily laden and was so low in the water that waves were constantly breaking over her bows. Even our top-quality waterproofs couldn't keep the water out and we were soaked through and cold.

'On each trip we spent fifteen continuous days actually fishing. The trawl was put out for five or six hours, which was when we could sleep and feed, provided that all the previous catch had been gutted, boxed and put in the hold. But sometimes the catch was so large that it was time to haul the next one by the time the last one had been dealt with.'

'And what did you eat out there?' I asked.

'Mainly corned beef hash. There was usually a huge pan of this in the galley, and you nipped in when you could to have a bowlful.'

'Didn't you eat some of the catch?'

'You must be joking. Fish …!

'Being a trawlerman was like enduring a cold wet hell continually for three weeks. I remember once, on my first trip, in February,

helping to get the cod-end of the net aboard. It was dark, raining and blowing a near gale, the ship was lurching about in the waves and I was wet and freezing cold. My mate said, 'Don't look up!' So I looked up. And all I could see, coming out of the black darkness, was a mass of white water crashing down on us. I held onto the net. Without that I would have been washed overboard and been lost. What a life. Just for a bit of cod!'

Harry Whiteside comes from a long line of inshore fishermen working from Warton and Freckleton on the north side of the Ribble estuary. Like so many similar Lancashire fishermen Harry has seen the collapse of the once huge cod, plaice, dab and sole stocks, and now makes a small income from netting salmon in the estuary. When he hangs up his net it is possible that his licence will not be re-let to a new generation of fishermen, for there is none to follow Harry.

We were out a couple of miles off Lytham when Harry suddenly broke out into a poem that he had composed. As he proclaimed, so the church bells of Lytham began to echo across the flat expanse of mud and water. It was as if I was witnessing the death knell of a once thriving fishing industry, ruined by European Common Fisheries legislation and incompetent fishery management here at home.

LEAN TIMES

There are no fish in the river,
  The children will all have to starve,
We've no food in the pantry,
  And we have no meat to carve.
The wife, she has no clothes to wear
  Her tear-filled eyes leak deep despair,
She'd sell her soul if she just dare
  When there are no fish in the river.

The paint is peeling off the wall,
  The ceiling has a great big hole.
Maybe soon I'll be upon the dole,
  For there are no fish in the river.

The river is deep and the river is wide,
  There are great banks of mud on either side,
And I've seen the time when grown men cried,
  There are no fish in the river!

In dead of night when black cloud sail
  Across a moon that is milky and pale,
I sit in my boat and rant and rail
  Because there are no fish in the river!

The faceless experts in ministerial halls
  Have charts and graphs but they know Sod All,
It is on us, not them, that the blunt axe will fall
  Because there are no fish left in the river.

And then the trusty lads will go no more to cast
  Their nets from Ribble's shore.
And the families they proudly kept
  Will join the bewildered and starving throngs
Crying, 'There are no fish in the world!'

GAME

'Four-and-twenty blackbirds were baked in a pie,
When the pie was open, the birds began to sing,
Oh! Wasn't that a dainty dish to set before the king!'

Traditional nursery rhyme

IT IS DIFFICULT FOR MOST MODERN Lancastrians to appreciate how much wild animals would have contributed to the diet of rural Lancastrians a hundred and more years ago. But when protein was in short supply, almost anything that swam, ran or flew was potential food. So blackbirds were indeed caught and baked in pies. So too were rooks and starlings (only the breasts, for in these the rest is very bitter), chaffinches, sparrows and thrushes (including the redwing and fieldfare that visit us in the winter). Those living close to the coast or fresh water marshes, that were widespread through the county into the eighteenth century, might catch waders like lapwing, curlew, golden plover, redshank and dunlin. Larger species, including wildfowl, grouse, partridge and pheasant, were the preserve of the lord of the manor and other wealthy people, and if a peasant was observed catching one of these it was forfeit to his superior.

After plucking and cleaning the birds were roasted or put into pies or stews. Small birds, however, could be put straight into a ball of clay and put into the red-hot embers of the fire. It has often been said that this was the way gypsies cooked hedgehogs. But the method would have been far more widespread than that. It was a traditional method of cooking used by all rural folk. When the bird or hedgehog was cooked, the hard clay was broken. Feathers, spines and skin would have stuck to the clay and the opened clay ball would reveal the perfectly cooked hot meat.

During the eighteenth century, as common land disappeared and large farms and country estates came to dominate rural Lancashire, so game became an important asset of the landowner. National game laws helped protect those assets by ensuring that the courts would treat poachers harshly. And the landowners benefited by catching or shooting the game themselves and selling it through the markets, or they charged large rents to those who wanted to enjoy shooting or hunting.

The large tracts of sand dunes between Southport and Crosby, to the west of Lytham (on which was built the town of St Annes), and east of Rossall Point (on which was built Fleetwood), were all rabbit warrens well into the nineteenth century. The owners of the dunes paid warreners to prevent poaching and if they caught anyone poaching they had them prosecuted for being 'in pursuit of coneys'. The warreners used ferrets to harvest a crop of rabbits in every month that has an 'r' in it (September to April) and the rabbit carcasses were sold as meat and the skins for the manufacture of felt.

Wild duck and geese were shot or trapped in nets wherever they gathered. Inland of Hale Point, though now politically in Cheshire, the most southerly place in the County Palatine of Lancaster, was dug a special pond. Five large tapering pipes made of willow and netting were constructed at each corner and any ducks alighting on the pond were decoyed into one of the pipes. When the ducks realised that it was a trap it was too late. Their necks were wrung and off to market they went. Between 1801 and 1825, 6,132 ducks were caught at Hale duck decoy. Those sitting on the right side of an aeroplane coming in to land at Liverpool Airport from the east (the usual approach in a westerly wind) may spot the old decoy pond, with its five arms that used to be covered by the pipes, just before landing.

‘SMALL BIRDS COULD BE PUT STRAIGHT INTO A BALL OF CLAY AND PUT INTO THE RED-HOT EMBERS OF THE FIRE’

Pantling for snipe and skylarks was described earlier (page 5). Large numbers of ducks and other waterside birds were caught with douker nets set below the high-water mark and flighting nets set on the marshes to catch birds flying at night.

Rabbits, waterfowl and waders such as curlew and lapwing, though good to eat, were not considered to be 'game', and they still aren't. Legally game includes hares and pheasants, partridges and grouse. Traditionally hares were coursed by wealthy landowners who made bets with each other as to whose greyhound was the best coursing dog. Pheasants, partridges and red grouse are shot mainly using the 'battue' system imported from the continent by Prince Albert, husband to Queen Victoria. The guns line up at one end of the wood, farmland or heather moor and beaters drive the birds over them. This is expensive shooting. In 2006 prices, £500–1000 is not excessive for a day's shooting and those who shoot them are handed a brace of birds to take home, the rest going to market.

And this is where the modern Lancastrian can benefit. Though some game birds, notably pheasants and red-legged partridges, are reared initially in pens they become truly 'free-range' as soon as they are released. They, together with the fully wild game, offer the choice of lean, flavoursome meat often at a price that is lower than the price of top-quality free-range chicken. Most of the county's markets sell rabbits, pheasants and mallard, sometimes partridge, grouse, teal, wigeon, woodcock and hares from October to February. In 2005–6, a brace of unplucked pheasants and partridges cost £3.50 and oven-ready birds £3.00 each. Great food if you know how to cook it properly.

> *WILD GAME OFFERS THE CHOICE OF LEAN FLAVOURSOME MEAT, OFTEN FOR LESS THAN A FREE RANGE CHICKEN*

Between the Norman Conquest and the reign of James I, Lancashire was noted for its royal deer forests where the deer were protected and forest laws harsh against those who tried to injure them. James broke up the forests and one result was that the two native deer, the red and roe, became almost extinct in the county. In the last fifty years or so, the roe has spread rapidly and it now occurs throughout. Its numbers have grown so large that it has become a pest species in some places, such as in parts of the Ribble and Hodder valleys, and many are culled every year. Sometimes you will see legs of roe for sale: they are delicious. Red deer, and the non-native sika and fallow deer, are not yet so widespread. However, red deer is farmed and its venison is frequently on sale. So too is the meat of farmed wild boars, a gamey form of pork.

The sad thing is that few families take advantage of the wide array of game that is available today.

The question of hanging and storing game

Many people have written that game should be hung to help tenderise the meat or to help develop the gamey taste of the meat. Personally I cannot see the point of leaving a dead bird hanging up by its neck in the garden shed until it is rotting and smells as if it is rotting. Properly hung meat (beef, lamb) is kept in a regulated cool environment, something that most of us do not have. Therefore it seems best to get the game either eaten or into the deep freeze as soon as possible.

If, like me, you buy most of your game remember that it will have been dead a few days when you get hold of it. Check all game carefully,

Free range guinea fowl are a type of cultivated game.

especially wild ducks. If the webs between their toes are hard and not soft and pliable, don't buy them. The birds (and hares and rabbits) that you might buy should not smell foul.

Sometimes the game dealer will skin rabbits and hares for you. All you need do then is to joint them and pack the joints in meal-sized lots in polythene bags in the freezer. To save the time in plucking and cleaning birds, I often buy them oven-ready and plonk them in the freezer in their packaging.

There are two easy ways of treating birds in full feather. Either take their breasts and discard everything else (that is mostly inedible anyway) or take a crown roast. I pluck a few feathers from the breast of the bird and if I can see more than one or two shot marks I take the breasts.

Cut a hole in the skin. Then pull the skin off the breast meat. Take a small very sharp knife and cut down on either side of the breastbone and continue cutting on either side until you have removed both breasts. That is so easy! Pack these in twos for making pâté or game parcels (page 127).

> **'TO SAVE THE TIME IN PLUCKING AND CLEANING BIRDS, BUY THEM OVEN-READY AND PLONK THEM IN THE FREEZER IN THEIR PACKAGING'**

If the breast meat shows little or no sign of damage then I take the crown roast.

Pluck the breasts and sides as far down as the wing and leg bases. Take a strong pair of kitchen scissors and cut along the sides into the body cavity below the breast meat. Cut back to the rear until the back part of the crown roast is completely severed. Now cut forward on either side, through the bones of the wing bases to the neck of the bird, again taking a line below the breast meat. Finally lift up the crown, freeing it from any other tissues. You now have the crown roast: the two breasts supported by the large breastbone. This can be roasted and the breasts carved, but reduce the roasting time by a third.

We eat game at least once a week throughout the year. For omnivorous humans it provides quality protein and a different flavour from the four main butcher meats of lamb, pork, beef and chicken.

Rabbit Pie

This was a very popular dish in the mining communities of Lancashire. In *The Road to Wigan Pier*, George Orwell described the poorest of families and by so doing implied that all mining families lived in squalor. They most certainly did not. Although miners spent their working lives deep underground, their bodies wracked by hard work and their lungs and eyes blackened by dust, when they were above ground a large proportion enjoyed the open air. They kept racing pigeons. They had their allotments. Some had ferrets and a whippet and they went rabbiting on the overgrown slag heaps.

A wild rabbit: agricultural pest, a gourmet's delight.

Although the Wigan–Leigh coalfield is no longer worked and miners there are a part of history, when friends who came from mining families there know that I will be visiting Bolton or Bury market they will often ask, 'Will you bring us back a rabbit?'

Make a pound of pastry and put that in the fridge to cool.

Joint the rabbit and take any extra bits such as bones (e.g. rib cage) and heart and boil them to make some stock. You can enrich the stock with a beef stock cube or a glass of red wine.

Take a pound of lean bacon, remove the rind and chop the bacon into small pieces.

Make some veal forcemeat stuffing by mixing together four ounces each of stale breadcrumbs and grated suet. Then mix in a heaped teaspoon of dried mixed herbs (or just dried thyme), a tablespoon of chopped parsley, a half-teaspoon of salt and finely grated lemon zest, some black pepper and a little grated nutmeg. Now mix in one large free-range egg and add enough milk so that the final mix will form balls that do not break apart easily. Make several forcemeat balls about one inch in diameter.

Line the bottom of a dish with half the pastry. Put in half the rabbit joints, and then scatter the forcemeat balls and bacon over. Add the rest of the rabbit joints. Pour in stock until the dish is three quarters full. Season with salt and pepper. Use the rest of the pastry to make a lid to cover the pie.

Put into a hot oven for ten minutes before tuning the oven down to moderate for about two hours.

'SOME HAD FERRETS AND
A WHIPPET AND THEY
WENT RABBITING ON THE
OVERGROWN SLAG HEAPS'

Rabbit Stew with Dumplings

An alternative to rabbit pie.

Chop a rabbit up into about six portions: two front legs, two hind legs and the rest of the carcass into two. Dust these with plain flour and fry until brown on all sides.

Put the rabbit pieces into a casserole dish with eight ounces of diced streaky bacon (preferably smoked), a large leek, onion, three carrots and two sticks of celery, all chopped up, and half a dozen button mushrooms. Pour in chicken stock (use a good stock cube) and a couple of tablespoons of mushroom ketchup. Add a bouquet garni or a teaspoon of dried mixed herbs. Season, cover and cook in a moderate oven for one hour.

Make some dumplings: mix four ounces of self-raising flour with two of suet, season and add some chopped herbs, and add water to produce a stiff dough. Roll into balls.

Turn the oven up to hot and if necessary add some boiling water to the stew if it seems to be drying out too much. Put in the dumplings and cook for a further ½ – ¾ hour, until the dumplings are brown on top.

Hare or Venison Casserole (or Pie)

Take all the meat off the bones and chop the meat into bite-sized cubes. The amount of meat you need depends, of course, on how many will be sitting down to dinner and you should aim for 4–6 ounces of game meat per person. As a rough guide, the meat from one hare will feed at least six people. To this meat add shin beef or stewing steak so that the final ratio will be four parts game meat to one part of beef. Put the meat in a large bowl and marinade it overnight with a bottle of red wine (an Aussie cabernet sauvignon or shiraz is ideal) and a couple of tablespoons of olive oil.

Boil the bones to make stock (or use a beef stock cube).

Drain the meat (save the liquid) and put in a large casserole dish, together with chopped up carrot, onion and a stick of celery. Add mixed herbs, salt and black pepper. Add liquid in the form of equal amounts of marinade and stock until the meat and vegetables are well covered. Cook in a hot oven for ten minutes and then turn down to moderate or moderate-low for three to four hours. Check that the casserole doesn't dry out: if it is doing so, add more stock/marinade. The key is to cook slowly to produce the tenderest meat.

A suet crust may be put over the meat and cooked during the last twenty minutes before serving. Or you could put some dumplings in to cook in the final twenty minutes.

This is not a recipe fixed in stone. Try other game meats if you have them. Some years ago, for a large dinner party, I managed to get eleven meats into this dish and I tried to have my friends name them. They included: red and roe venison, hare, rabbit, pheasant, grey and red-legged partridge, woodpigeon, red grouse and wild boar, plus, of course, stewing steak. Pigeon pie can be made in exactly the same way, using the breasts of woodpigeon plus stewing steak (large numbers of woodpigeons are shot in West Lancashire in February).

Game Parcels

This is a modification of Fred J. Taylor's wonderful way of cooking the breasts of any game bird, from pheasants to grouse, from mallard to teal.

First make a simple stuffing. Put some stale white bread in the food processor and whiz until you have breadcrumbs. Now add a little onion and give it another whiz. Add the finely grated zest and the juice of lemon, lime or orange, salt and pepper and some mixed dry herbs and give a final whiz.

Take a pack of smoked pancetta (Fred used streaky bacon) and arrange on a baking tray so that the slices form a long rectangle, each slice overlapping slightly with the one before. Arrange half the breasts along the centre of the pancetta rectangle. Put a thin layer of stuffing over these breasts and arrange the other breasts on top. Now fold the loose ends of the pancetta slices over until all the breasts and stuffing are enclosed. Turn the parcel over so that the cut ends are underneath. Place in a moderately hot oven and cook until the pancetta is brown and crisp. As a general guide, a small 'one-man' parcel containing two partridge breasts will take about twenty minutes, whereas a larger parcel containing four pheasant or mallard breasts will take about 45 minutes to cook.

These can be eaten hot, straight from the oven. Or you can wrap them in kitchen foil and have them cold, sliced in a sandwich or eaten whole with salad at a picnic.

Roast Game

The important thing to remember about roasting game is that, with the exception of pheasants, game is very lean and does not contain the fats that keep the meat of roast lamb or beef tender and moist. Cook game for too long and it will be tough. Some recipe books tell us that game should be cooked rare (i.e. not fully cooked) so that it will be moist. For those who, like me, detest very rare steaks and other meats, there is another solution to the problem of how to get game roasted well without it being dry and tough.

Rub butter over the bird, or rabbit, or hare, or leg or haunch of venison. Then, either wrap in streaky bacon (ideal for smaller birds up to the size of pheasant and mallard) or wrap well in kitchen foil. Put in a hot oven for ten minutes, turning the oven down to moderately hot for the remainder of the cooking time. If using kitchen foil, expose the meat for the last ten to fifteen minutes.

Approximate cooking times: snipe 15 minutes, woodcock and teal 25 minutes, partridge and wigeon 30 minutes, pheasant and mallard 40–45 minutes, rabbit 1–1½ hours, hare up to 2 hours, venison allow 30 minutes per pound.

Wild geese (feral Canada and greylag breed in Lancashire, while up to 30,000 pink-footed geese visit from Iceland for the winter) may be shot but not sold under British law. Sometimes a friendly wildfowler sends one my way from the Ribble estuary or Morecambe Bay. Wild geese are said to be too tough to eat. This is not so. The point is that they must be cooked very slowly.

Snipe being
caught by pantling
(see introduction).

Stuff the goose with a good stuffing (see page 127) and put it on two large pieces of kitchen foil. Rub butter over the breast of the bird and then, just as you pull up the sides of the tin foil, pour in a wine glass full of water or white wine. Parcel the bird in the two sheets of foil so that no steam can escape. Put the parcel in a roasting tin and put in a moderate to slow oven for about three hours. Take out of the oven and remove the foil. Put the bird back in the roasting tin and baste well with the fluid from the foil parcel. Roast in a moderately hot oven until the skin is nice and brown. Carve thin slices and serve with the stuffing.

'TAKE YOUR SMELLY DUCK AND MARINADE IT IN FULL CREAM MILK OVERNIGHT'

You may like to use this method whenever you suspect the game is an old bird and might be on the tough side.

FISHY DUCK

Note on game that smells 'fishy': Dick Shelton is a great wildfowler and he gave me the following tip to rid wild ducks and geese of the fishy smell and/or taste that they sometimes have. The problem is a foul smelling chemical that happens to be lipophilic. That means that the chemical molecules readily attach onto fat droplets. So take your smelly duck and marinade it in full cream milk overnight. The fat droplets in the milk will pick up the smelly chemical. Rinse the duck with cold water and cook. Hey, presto! A lovely, un-fishy duck!

Incidentally, it is a similar chemical that gives brassicas like cauliflower and cabbage their characteristic smell, which can stink the house out when you are cooking them. Add a tablespoon of full fat milk to the pan and the stench will be reduced, even prevented.

Kathy Falkus's Game Pâté

Roast two pheasants or mallard or their equivalent (e.g. four teal or woodpigeons) in a hot oven for twenty minutes. Carefully remove the breasts and slice. Carefully remove the meat from the legs. Then gather any scraps of meat left on the skeleton.

Make a forcemeat by mincing 1½lbs of belly of pork with any scraps of meat from the birds (the butcher may do this for you, or you might blitz it in the food processor if you haven't got a mincing machine). Add one crushed garlic clove, fifteen crushed peppercorns, two teaspoons of salt and flavourings. Mix well (or whiz with the food processor). Then add two beaten eggs and mix again.

The flavourings can be:

1. 10 crushed juniper berries, plus half a wine glass of Madeira.

2. The zest of two oranges, the juice of one orange and a third of a wine glass of Cointreau.

3. 6 crushed juniper berries, plus a quarter pint of sweet sherry or sherry and brandy mixed.

Take ½lb of salt pork and cut into small dice.

Line a terrine with rashers of streaky bacon (or smoked pancetta). Next put in a layer of forcemeat then a layer of the lean part-roast meat and diced salt pork, followed by a layer of forcemeat and then a layer of lean meat and diced salt pork, finishing off with a layer of forcemeat. Decorate the top with juniper berries and bay leaves. Put the terrine in a roasting tin and add water to the tin so that it comes just over half way up the sides of the terrine. Put in a moderate-slow oven for 1½ hours.

When cooked, cover the pâté with greaseproof paper and weight it down gently with, say, small cans of baked beans or their equivalent.

This will keep for a week or two in a cold pantry or fridge.

Kathy Falkus was a farmer's daughter and a great country cook. She had just started working on a country cook book when she died.

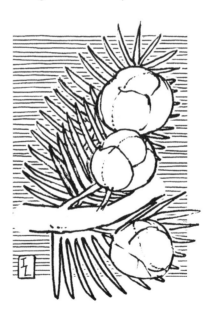

PUDDINGS AND CAKES

'The poor man's gout arises from too little, or too poor food, causing an impoverished state of the system; the remedy (were such possible) would be to exchange tables with the rich man, this (perhaps) not being possible the substitute is: Live well on good substantial food, the very best you can afford, with, if you can afford it, an occasional glass of good port wine, or Guinness's (harp label) stout.'

Nicholas Culpeper, *The British Herbal and Family Physician*, n.d.

THE MOST INTERESTING FEATURE that came out of my researches into Lancashire food was the immense importance of sweet foods, mainly cakes and puddings, but also sweets. For instance, an old notebook, dating from the early years of the twentieth century (perhaps a little earlier), in which the late Annie Warburton of Hindley recorded her own recipes, includes 26 cakes and puddings, her own mix of mincemeat, a recipe for beetroot wine, and three recipes for jam. There is not one meat or vegetable recipe.

The virtue of rich cakes and heavy puddings is now considered a vice! They were packed with calories in the form of dried fruits, sugar and fat (lard or suet). But in those days when there was no central heating the body had to generate lots of heat, especially in winter. Only the well off had cars, and everyone else walked, perhaps only to the tram or bus stop, but they still walked. It was nothing for a boy or girl to walk a mile each way to school. Children then needed lots of calories. Contrast that with mothers' school-runs of today.

And work then was far more physical. There were no automatic washing machines. On Monday the week's wash was soaked in the dolly-tub, then given either a good rubbing on the washboard or a good scrubbing. It was then manhandled into the sink for rinsing before being squeezed through the mangle and hung out to dry. No automatic spinning or tumble-drying then! Monday's washing and Tuesday's ironing was hard work and it needed lots of fuel in the diet.

Even shopping was more demanding. Today most of us drive to the supermarket, gather our purchases in a trolley, put them into the car and later carry them into the kitchen packed in small polythene bags. Then womenfolk walked to the grocers, greengrocers and butchers for the weekly shop. They filled one or two large bags and, thus laden down, they walked back home. Even the shopkeepers worked much harder then, for they moved around the shop to collect the things that their customers wanted to buy. They didn't sit on padded seats at checkouts!

> **6** WHAT WAS ONCE CONSIDERED THE VIRTUE OF RICH CAKES AND PUDDINGS IS NOW CONSIDERED A VICE **9**

And, for most people then, work meant work. Lancashire miners won coal underground with pick and shovel. Mill hands stood at their looms and often each worker had several machines to look after and therefore walked great distances in the course of a day's work. Holes in roads and the trenches for the footings of new buildings were then dug with pick and spade, for the JCB had yet to be invented. Today most 'workers' sit at desks in centrally heated offices and use upwards of a thousand calories a day less. Someone suggested that male office workers need about 2500 calories a day while women need about 2000 calories. For working people in 1906 the figures would have been closer to 5500 and 4000 calories.

No wonder that eating rich cakes and puddings fell out of favour other than for special occasions. And little wonder that today so many people, including small children, are grossly overweight.

Nevertheless, cakes and puddings *are* an important flavour of Lancashire and we should still enjoy them, in moderation, for special occasions, or on those cold winter evenings after a long day of physically hard work.

Cakes

Cakes have many virtues. They keep better than puddings. They can be cut up so that a slice can be taken out and eaten as part of a packed-lunch and children can have a piece of cake (rather than the e-number-loaded confectionary sold at the corner shop) after school. If someone calls, provided that you have a cake in the tin, you can offer them tea and cake. The following are some of the more famous Lancashire cakes.

Bury Simnel Cake

Note that this cake should not be confused with the rich fruitcake that has a layer of marzipan through the centre and also called Simnel cake. This is a Lancashire recipe and, though reputed to have been invented in Bury, it appears in notes from elsewhere in the county including Leigh–Wigan (where it was 'Symnol Cake').

> Rub six ounces of cooking fat (lard or butter or 50% each of lard and butter) into a pound of plain flour. This is easily done with the modern food processor: blitz it on high speed for a few seconds.
>
> Then stir in ten ounces of sugar, eight ounces each of currants and sultanas, four ounces each of candied peel and ground almonds, and a teaspoon each of nutmeg and cinnamon.
>
> Mix in two large free-range eggs and just enough milk to produce very stiff dough. Shape the dough into a ball, flatten one side and then put it flat side down on a lightly oiled baking tray. Brush the top with milk. Bake in a moderately hot oven for about one hour, until a fine knitting needle inserted into the centre comes out clean. Allow to cool on a wire rack.

Delicious sliced and spread with a little butter.

One variation of the Simnel cake theme dates from the mid 1700s and is clearly meant for quite a large party.

> First of all, mix ¾lb of fresh yeast with a little sugar and water and put in a warm place.
>
> Take five pounds of plain flour and mix in one pound of butter. Now add four pounds of currants, a pound of sugar, half a pound of candied peel, half a pound of chopped almonds, half an ounce of cinnamon and quarter of an ounce of nutmeg. Then mix in ten eggs, half a pint of single cream and the yeast culture.

Now leave the big, rich, fruity dough to rise in a warm place overnight. Before baking put the dough on a large greased baking tray and mould it so that there is a higher peak in the middle with a ditch-like hollow around the peak and a higher ridge around the outside. After cooking in a hot oven, thick syrup is poured into the 'ditch' and the entire cake sprinkled with sugar. People help themselves to this by pulling off a helping that was called 'a knob' of Simnel cake.

Incidentally, Simnel cake was eaten on Simnel Sunday in mid Lent, now called 'Mothering Sunday'.

Bun Loaf

This sweet bread was made on baking day when mother (in my family's case, grandmother) baked the week's bread. Most dough would go to make bread, but some was kept back for bun loaf.

First of all, start off the yeast. Into a bowl mix ¼ pint of luke water, a teaspoon each of bread flour and sugar, and either a teaspoonful of dry yeast or ¼ oz of fresh yeast. Put the bowl into a warm place.

Sift 1½ lb of white bread flour into a bowl and rub in ½ oz of lard. Then add the yeast culture and a level tablespoon of salt and mix in. Add extra milk, or water, or a milk/water mix a little at a time until you have a soft dough that does not stick easily to your hands. Put the ball of dough onto a floured surface and knead until the dough is soft and elastic. Put back in the bowl, cover with a cloth and leave to rise in a warm place until the dough has doubled in size (this will take about 1½ hours). Then put the dough back on the floured surface and knead once more, before kneading in 14 oz of mixed dry fruits, such as six ounces each of currants and sultanas and two ounces of candied peel.

Divide the dough into two and form into loaves that fit oiled, one-pound bread tins. Put the two tins, covered with a dry cloth, in a warm place until the dough has doubled in size. Then bake in a moderately hot oven for 35 minutes. Turn them out onto a wire rack and let them cool before slicing and spreading with butter.

Although bread with white wheat flour was developed elsewhere in England (see page 33), this sweet version was devised in Lancashire.

Cracknells

This is a simple crisp biscuit that can be sweetened by the addition of sugar, enriched by the addition of a little dried fruit, or enjoyed in its basic form (perhaps with some Lancashire cheese).

> Rub two ounces of lard into half a pound of plain flour. Then mix in half an ounce of baking powder and quarter of a pint of warmed milk. (Note that the easiest way of doing this today is with a food processor.)
>
> Knead well on a floured surface, then roll out and, using a three-inch cutter, form biscuits. Put them on a greased baking tray and cook until golden brown in a moderate oven.

Cracknells are very old, the Oxford English Dictionary tracing the term back to 1440, when 'Brede twyys bakyn' was called 'krakenelle'. Bread that was twice baked meant an unleavened dough as we have here, baked until it was very crisp and golden-brown, as we also have here.

Goosnargh Cakes

Goosnargh is a scattered village west of Longridge and a few miles north of Preston made famous by this biscuity confection.

> Mix well ten ounces of plain flour with eight ounces of butter, and then mix in two ounces of caster sugar, a teaspoonful of caraway seeds and half a teaspoon of ground coriander. The easiest way of doing this is with the food processor.
>
> Put on a floured surface and roll out to about a quarter of an inch thickness, and use a three-inch pastry cutter to produce the uncooked cakes. Dust the top with extra caster sugar and bake in a slow oven for about 40 minutes until firm and cooked, but still very pale in colour. Put on a wire rack to cool, dusting extra caster sugar over the top.

Eccles Cakes, Chorley Cakes, Lancashire Cakes etc

Lancashire is home to the pastry, sugar and currant cake, and some towns in Lancashire became famous for their own recipe. We will start off with the Eccles cake because it is so